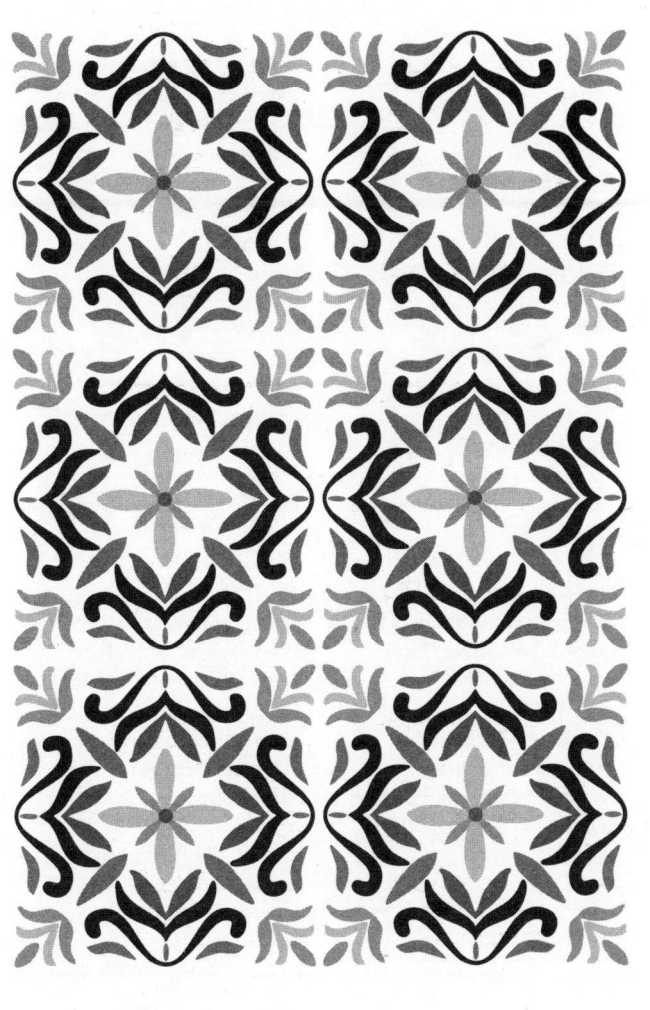

First published in Great Britain in 2026 by Hamlyn, an imprint of Octopus Publishing Group Ltd, Carmelite House, 50 Victoria Embankment London EC4Y 0DZ www.octopusbooks.co.uk

An Hachette UK Company www.hachette.co.uk

The authorized representative in the EEA is Hachette Ireland, 8 Castlecourt Centre, Dublin 15, D15 XTP3, Ireland (email: info@hbgi.ie)

Copyright © Octopus Publishing Group Ltd 2026

Distributed in the US by Hachette Book Group, 1290 Avenue of the Americas, 4th and 5th Floors, New York, NY 10104

Distributed in Canada by Canadian Manda Group, 664 Annette St., Toronto, Ontario, Canada M6S 2C8

ISBN 978-0-60064-015-8
eISBN 978-0-60064-021-9

A CIP catalogue record for this book is available from the British Library.

Printed and bound in Great Britian.

10 9 8 7 6 5 4 3 2 1

Publisher: Lucy Pessell
Cover Designer: Isobel Platt
Senior Designer: Alicia House
Senior Project Editor: Katie Button
Assistant Editor: Samina Rahman
Production Manager:
Allison Gonsalves

This FSC® label means that materials used for the product have been responsibly sourced.

MIX
Paper | Supporting
responsible forestry
FSC® C104740
www.fsc.org

RECIPES FOR
Summer

A Collection of Timeless
and Trusted Recipes

hamlyn

Contents

Introduction

As the weather warms, we crave light and refreshing tastes and bright and vibrant plates that can be enjoyed at home or al fresco.

Summer is the season for impromptu picnics in the park, light lunches in the sun and gatherings that go long into the evenings. It's also the time to let the culinary vibes of far-flung places shine through our cooking so that we're transported to our favourite tapas bar or souvlaki stand.

From small plates that bring style and sophistication to a lunch, salads and sides to complement whatever's on the grill, to mains that showcase the season's riot of fresh produce, here are over 80 recipes to help you celebrate the joys of summer dining.

The
Basics

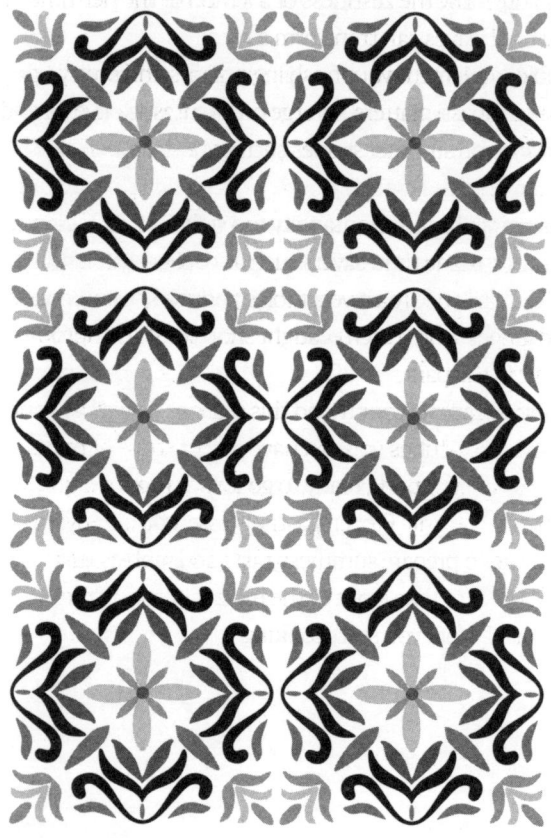

Being prepared

Summer is the height of the growing season and stores and market stalls are bursting with fresh produce so try to make the most of it. Many of the recipes in this book have one or two strong flavours, which serve to bring the dish to life. It's amazing how the zestiness of a lemon or the perfume of a few basil leaves can transform a meal.

To complement your fresh ingredients and pretty-up your antipasti platters, splurge on a fantastic olive oil and stock up on summer staples such as pesto, tapenades and pine nuts.

Summer brings spontaneity too so be on the look out for ready-made time-savers such as cooked rice, lentils and pulses, deli-style roast vegetables and ready-minced garlic and ginger so you aren't caught short for that impromptu picnic in the park.

Your freezer is your friend this season. As well as your hoard of ice-cubes you can have precut strips of meat, such as beef or pork, ready to go for stir-fries or a quick sizzle on the grill. Frozen pastry is essential for anyone wanting to prepare summery tarts and nibbles: just remember to take it out of the freezer in good time to thaw before you start cooking.

Store-cupboard essentials

One of the best ways of making life easy in the kitchen is to have a well-stocked store cupboard and freezer, so you need to buy just one or two items – fresh fish or meat, or some seasonal vegetables – and combine them with staples such as rice and noodles, and some well-flavoured spices or ready-made sauces.

Pulses, lentils & beans

Cans of precooked beans and lentils can be quickly heated through to make a simple meal substantial and filling. Experiment with different types. For example, borlotti beans are pretty and speckled when dried and light brown once cooked. Cannellini beans are a similar size to kidney beans but pale in colour.

Pasta, noodles, grains & rice

Pasta takes little time to cook and can be used to accompany a wide range of dishes. Rice takes longer to cook, but it is possible to buy precooked rice. Cellophane, rice and udon noodles take just a few minutes to prepare and can be added to soups and stir-fries to create filling, nourishing dishes.

Herbs & spices

Make sure your shelves are well stocked with spices and herbs. It is also easy to keep a few herbs – basil, parsley and coriander – growing on the kitchen windowsill, so that you can add a few freshly chopped leaves to garnish finished dishes.

Sauces & pastes

If you like to cook Eastern dishes, you will probably already have bottles of soy sauce and fish sauce on your shelves.

Tahini is a thick paste made from hulled, roasted sesame seeds, and it is a key ingredient in hummus. You will find tahini in most supermarkets or Middle Eastern food stores.

Storage

Some recipes can be frozen, jarred or saved for later. If you want to keep sauces, dressings or preserves in a jar, make sure to wash the jars in hot soapy water and to sterilize all jars and screw-top lids after washing and just before filling. Rinse well with hot water to remove any soapy residues, drain and then stand them in a roasting tin. Warm in a preheated oven set to 160°C (325°F), Gas Mark 3, for 10 minutes.

Alternatively, wash in a dishwasher and use while still warm, but make sure they are perfectly dry before filling.

Small Plates & Sides

Caesar Salad

SERVES 4
PREPARATION TIME 20 minutes
COOKING TIME 5 minutes

1 garlic clove, crushed
4 anchovy fillets in oil,
    drained and chopped
juice of 1 lemon
1–2 teaspoons Dijon mustard
1 egg yolk
200 ml (7 fl oz) olive oil

vegetable oil, for frying
3 slices of white bread,
    cut into cubes
1 cos lettuce, washed and torn
    into pieces
3 tablespoons grated
    Parmesan
pepper

Put the garlic, anchovies, lemon juice, mustard and egg yolk in a small bowl and sprinkle with pepper. Mix well until combined. Slowly drizzle in the olive oil, mixing all the time to make a thick, creamy dressing. If the dressing is too thick, add a little water.

Heat the vegetable oil in a frying pan. Test with one of the bread cubes to see if it is hot enough; if the bread sizzles, add the rest of the cubes, turning them when they are golden brown, then drain on kitchen paper.

Put the lettuce into a large bowl, pour on the dressing and sprinkle with 2 tablespoons of the Parmesan; mix well. Top with the croûtons and the remaining Parmesan and serve.

Spinach, Avocado & Bacon Salad

SERVES 4
PREPARATION TIME 15 minutes
COOKING TIME 10 minutes

FOR THE DRESSING

3 tablespoons balsamic
  vinegar
1 teaspoon light soft
  brown sugar
1 teaspoon Dijon mustard
125 ml (4 fl oz) olive oil
1 tablespoon finely chopped
  walnuts, plus extra to
  garnish (optional)
1 tablespoon chopped
  parsley or basil
salt and pepper

FOR THE SALAD

1 ripe avocado, halved, peeled
  and pitted
2 tablespoons lemon juice
500 g (1 lb) baby spinach
  leaves
small bunch of spring onions,
  shredded into long, thin
  strips
2 tablespoons vegetable oil
4 rindless back bacon
  rashers, chopped
1 garlic clove, crushed

Make the dressing. Mix the vinegar, sugar and mustard in a bowl. Add a dash of salt and pepper, then slowly whisk in the oil. Stir the walnuts and herbs into the dressing and add more salt and pepper if needed.

Make the salad. Chop the avocado into cubes and sprinkle with the lemon juice to stop it going brown.

Put the spinach leaves in a bowl together with the spring onions and avocado.

Heat the oil in a frying pan and fry the bacon and the garlic until crisp and brown, then drain on kitchen paper. Scatter over the spinach mixture.

Drizzle some of the dressing over the salad, toss gently and serve straight away, garnished with extra walnut pieces, if liked.

Tricolore Couscous Salad

SERVES 4
PREPARATION TIME 10 minutes
COOKING TIME 10 minutes

200 g (7 oz) couscous
300 ml (½ pint) hot vegetable stock or boiling water
250 g (8 oz) cherry tomatoes, halved
2 avocados, peeled, stoned and chopped
150 g (5 oz) mozzarella, chopped
handful of rocket leaves

FOR THE DRESSING
2 tablespoons ready-made fresh green pesto
1 tablespoon lemon juice
4 tablespoons extra virgin olive oil
salt and pepper

Mix the couscous and stock or boiling water together in a bowl, then cover with a plate and leave for 10 minutes.

Make the dressing. Mix the pesto with the lemon juice and season, then gradually mix in the oil. Pour over the couscous and mix with a fork.

Add the tomatoes, avocados and mozzarella to the couscous, mix well, then lightly stir in the rocket.

Serrano Ham, Fig & Rocket Salad

SERVES 4–6

PREPARATION TIME 10 minutes

FOR THE DRESSING
1 tablespoon finely chopped
   shallot
1 thyme sprig, leaves stripped
   and finely chopped
1 tablespoon sherry vinegar
3 tablespoons extra virgin
   olive oil
salt and pepper

FOR THE SALAD
100 g (3½ oz) rocket leaves
4 figs, halved or quartered
   if large
150 g (5 oz) Serrano ham,
   sliced

Make the dressing. Mix together the shallot, thyme and vinegar in a bowl. Season well, then whisk in the oil until well combined.

Toss the rocket with a little of the dressing, then arrange on a serving plate with the figs and ham. Drizzle over the remaining dressing and serve.

Soured Cucumber Salad with Goats' Curd

SERVES 4
PREPARATION TIME 5 minutes
COOKING TIME 5 minutes + cooling & standing

FOR THE CUCUMBERS
200 ml (7 fl oz) white wine
    vinegar
2 tablespoons caster sugar
1 tablespoon mustard seeds
1 teaspoon pink peppercorns
2 baby cucumbers, chopped
    into wedges
1 teaspoon sea salt
50 g (2 oz) dill

FOR THE MATCHA SALT
1 tablespoon sea salt flakes
½ teaspoon matcha powder

TO SERVE
120 g (4 oz) goats' curd
4 slices of wholemeal bread
20 g (¾ oz) dill

Prepare the cucumbers. Heat the vinegar, sugar, mustard seeds and peppercorns in a saucepan, stirring until the sugar has dissolved. Set aside to cool.

Place the cucumber in a colander and toss with the salt. Leave to stand for 15 minutes before transferring to a sterilized jar (see page 9) along with the dill. Pour over the cooled vinegar and sugar solution and seal with an airtight lid. The cucumbers will be sour enough to eat a day later, but will keep for up to a month in the refrigerator, becoming more sour over time.

Combine the salt and matcha powder in a small bowl.

To serve, spread the goats' curd on a serving plate and arrange the cucumber wedges on top. Toast the bread and finish by sprinkling over the matcha salt, dill and a little pickling liquor.

New Potato Salad with Turmeric Tahini Dressing

SERVES 2
PREPARATION TIME 10 minutes
COOKING TIME 10–20 minutes

500 g (1 lb) new potatoes, washed
leaves from ½ bunch of mint
4 spring onions, thinly sliced on the diagonal
1 teaspoon sumac
sea salt and ground black pepper

FOR THE DRESSING
80 g (3 oz) tahini
juice of 1 lemon
30 ml (1 fl oz) extra virgin olive oil
2 tablespoons water
1 teaspoon ground turmeric

Put the potatoes in a large saucepan and add enough cold water to cover them fully. Add a small handful of salt and 2 sprigs of the mint before covering with a lid. Place over a high heat and bring to the boil. Reduce the heat slightly and allow to simmer until the potatoes are easily pierced with a sharp knife. Drain and allow to cool slightly – it's best to serve the salad warm but not piping hot.

In the meantime, make the dressing. Put all the ingredients into a large bowl and whisk until smooth. If it looks like the oil is separating, just whisk in 1 tablespoon of water at a time until the dressing is thick and glossy. Season with a generous pinch of salt and pepper.

Toss the warm potatoes in the dressing, add the remaining mint leaves and the spring onions and mix until thoroughly combined. Tip into a serving bowl and sprinkle the sumac evenly over the top.

Wild Rice, Crab & Mango Salad

SERVES 4
PREPARATION TIME 15 minutes
COOKING TIME 30 minutes

200 g (7 oz) mixed wild and basmati rice

1 tablespoon finely chopped red onion

1 teaspoon root ginger, peeled and finely chopped

1 red chilli, finely chopped

3 tablespoons olive oil

finely grated rind and juice of 1 lime

large handful of coriander, chopped

1 mango, peeled, stoned and chopped

150 g (5 oz) cooked fresh crabmeat

Bring a large saucepan of lightly salted water to the boil, add the rice and cook for 25 minutes, or according to the instructions on the packet until just tender. Drain and rinse under cold running water to cool.

Meanwhile, mix the onion with the ginger, chilli, oil and the rind and juice of the lime in a large bowl.

Add the rice, coriander, mango and crabmeat, stir well and serve.

Mexican-Style Seafood Cocktail

SERVES 4
PREPARATION TIME 10 minutes + standing
COOKING TIME 10 minutes

150 g (5 oz) raw prawns, peeled
150 g (5 oz) scallops, shelled and cleaned
300 ml (½ pint) tomato juice
1 tablespoon tomato ketchup
lime juice, to taste
Tabasco sauce, to taste
1 ripe avocado, stoned, peeled and chopped
1 spring onion, sliced
handful of coriander, chopped

Place the prawns in a bowl, pour over boiling water to cover and leave for 2 minutes. Add the scallops, adding a little more boiling water, and leave for a further 3 minutes, then drain.

Mix the tomato juice, ketchup, a good squeeze of lime juice and Tabasco sauce, to taste, together. Add the prawns and scallops to the sauce, stir well and leave to stand for 10 minutes.

Spoon into serving bowls. Top with the avocado, spring onion and coriander.

Parmesan &
Tomato Tarts

MAKES 24
PREPARATION TIME 30 minutes + chilling
COOKING TIME 18–20 minutes

FOR THE PASTRY
175 g (6 oz) plain flour, plus
    extra for dusting
75 g (3 oz) butter, diced
2 tablespoons chopped basil
2 tablespoons cold water

FOR THE FILLING
2 eggs
150 ml (¼ pint) milk
50 g (2 oz) Parmesan, finely
    grated
3 spring onions, finely
    chopped
12 small cherry tomatoes,
    halved
salt and pepper
tiny basil leaves, to garnish

Make the pastry. Add the flour, a little salt and pepper and the butter to a mixing bowl, then rub in the butter with your fingertips or using an electric mixer until you have fine crumbs. Add the basil, then mix in enough water to form a soft but not sticky dough.

Knead the pastry lightly, then roll it out thinly on a lightly floured surface. Stamp out 24 x 6 cm (2½ inch) circles with a plain biscuit cutter, then press into the buttered sections of 2 × 12-hole mini muffin tins, rerolling the trimmings as needed. Chill for 15 minutes.

Make the filling. Fork the eggs and milk together in a · bowl. Add the Parmesan, spring onions and a little salt and pepper and mix well. Spoon into the pastry casings, then add a tomato half to each one.

Bake in a preheated oven, 180°C (350°F), Gas Mark 4, for 18–20 minutes until golden and the filling is just set. Leave to stand for 10 minutes, then loosen the edges of the tarts and remove from the tins. Garnish with tiny basil leaves just before serving.

Smoked Salmon & Mint Pea Tarts

MAKES 6
PREPARATION TIME 20 minutes
COOKING TIME 15 minutes

500 g (1 lb) ready-made
  puff pastry
flour, for dusting
25 g (1 oz) butter
6 spring onions, thinly sliced
250 g (8 oz) frozen peas,
  defrosted

2 Little Gem lettuces,
  thickly sliced
2 tablespoons chopped mint
250 g (8 oz) crème fraîche
200 g (7 oz) smoked salmon
salt and pepper

Cut the pastry into 6 pieces, then roll each piece out on a lightly floured surface and trim to a 15 cm (6 inch) circle. Transfer the pastry rounds to 2 large, lightly oiled baking sheets. To make the crust, lightly score a border 2.5 cm (1 inch) from the edge of the pastry round and prick all over the middle with a fork. Repeat with the other rounds.

Bake in a preheated oven, 200°C (400°F), Gas Mark 6, for 10 minutes until well risen. Press down the centre and cook for a further 5 minutes until the tart cases are crisp and golden.

Meanwhile, heat the butter in a frying pan, then add the spring onions and fry until softened. Add the peas and cook for a few minutes until hot, add the lettuce and cook for 30 seconds, then stir in the mint, crème fraîche and salt and pepper.

Spoon the pea mixture into the hot tart cases and arrange the smoked salmon in folds on top. Sprinkle with a little extra pepper and serve at once with a green salad.

Pizza Puff Pies

MAKES 6
PREPARATION TIME 25 minutes
COOKING TIME 40 minutes

1 tablespoon olive oil
1 onion, chopped
1 garlic clove, finely chopped
400 g (13 oz) can chopped
　tomatoes
1 teaspoon caster sugar
500 g (1 lb) ready-made puff
　pastry, defrosted if frozen

flour, for dusting
small bunch of basil
125 g (4 oz) mozzarella,
　drained
6 pitted black olives (optional)
salt and pepper
olive oil, to serve (optional)

Heat the oil in a saucepan, add the onion and fry for 5 minutes until softened. Add the garlic, tomatoes and sugar, and season with salt and pepper. Cover and simmer gently for 15 minutes, stirring from time to time until the sauce has thickened. Leave to cool slightly.

Cut the pastry into 6, then roll out each piece on a lightly floured surface and trim to a 15 cm (6 inch) circle using a saucer as a guide. Press each pastry circle into the base of a lightly oiled metal Yorkshire pudding tin or tart tin, 10 cm (4 inches) in diameter, 2.5 cm (1 inch) deep, and press the pastry at intervals to the sides of the tin to give a wavy edge.

Reserve half the smaller basil leaves for garnish, tear the larger leaves into pieces and stir into the sauce. Divide the sauce between the cases and spread into an even layer. Cut the mozzarella into 6 slices and add a slice to each pie. Sprinkle with a little salt and pepper, and add an olive to each, if using.

Bake in a preheated oven, 200°C (400°F), Gas Mark 6, for 20 minutes until the pastry is crisp and golden. Leave to cool for 5 minutes, then turn out. Drizzle with a little oil, if liked, sprinkle with the remaining basil leaves and serve warm with a green salad.

Goats' Cheese, Pear & Pistachio Melts

SERVES 4
PREPARATION TIME 10 minutes
COOKING TIME 2 minutes

4 large slices of sourdough
   bread
2 garlic cloves, halved
1 tablespoon olive oil
1 pear, thinly sliced
100 g (3½ oz) pistachio nuts,
   chopped
2 small crottin de chèvre,
   thinly sliced
pepper

Rub the bread with the garlic cloves and drizzle each with the oil.

Arrange the pear over the bread. Scatter over the pistachio nuts, cover with slices of chèvre and a little pepper.

Melt under a hot grill for 2 minutes and serve with a radicchio salad.

Brie & Thyme Melts

SERVES 4
PREPARATION TIME 5 minutes
COOKING TIME 10 minutes

1 ciabatta-style loaf, cut in half horizontally
6 tablespoons onion or caramelized onion chutney

200 g (7 oz) Brie or Camembert, sliced
1 teaspoon dried thyme
4 teaspoons chilli, garlic or basil oil

Cut the 2 pieces of bread in half to give 4 portions. Arrange, cut-side up, on a baking sheet and spread each piece with the onion chutney.

Lay the cheese slices on top and sprinkle with the thyme. Drizzle with the flavoured oil and cook under a preheated hot grill for 3–4 minutes until the cheese begins to melt. Serve immediately with a tomato salad, if liked.

Blue Cheese Soufflé

SERVES 6
PREPARATION TIME 10 minutes
COOKING TIME 30 minutes

75 g (3 oz) crustless
   sourdough bread,
   cut into chunks
250 ml (8 fl oz) milk
150 g (5 oz) blue cheese,
   crumbled
50 g (2 oz) butter, softened,
   plus extra for greasing
4 eggs, separated

1 tablespoon white wine
   vinegar
3 tablespoons olive oil
1 teaspoon walnut oil
1 red apple, cored and
   thinly sliced
handful of rocket leaves
salt and pepper

Put the bread in a bowl and pour over the milk. Leave to soak for 5 minutes, then squeeze any excess milk. Transfer the bread to a food processor or blender with the cheese, butter and egg yolks and blend until smooth. Season to taste.

Whisk the egg whites in a large, grease-free bowl until stiff peaks form. Stir a large spoonful into the cheese mixture, then carefully fold in the remainder, half at a time.

Spoon the mixture into 6 x 150 ml (¼ pint) well-greased ramekins and bake in a preheated oven, 220°C (425°F), Gas Mark 7, for 10–15 minutes until puffed and golden.

Meanwhile, whisk together the vinegar, olive oil and walnut oil and season to taste. Toss together with the apple and rocket leaves.

Serve the soufflés immediately with the dressed rocket and apple alongside.

Asparagus Mimosa

SERVES 4
PREPARATION TIME 5 minutes
COOKING TIME 20 minutes

6 quails' or 2 hens' eggs
200 g (7 oz) asparagus spears, trimmed
1 teaspoon Dijon mustard
1 tablespoon white wine vinegar

1 tablespoon single cream
75 ml (3 fl oz) olive oil
1 tablespoon drained capers
50 g (2 oz) pitted black olives, chopped
salt and pepper

Bring a saucepan of water to the boil and gently lower in the eggs. Cook the quails' eggs for 5 minutes or the hens' eggs for 8 minutes. Remove from the pan and cool under cold running water.

Meanwhile, cook the asparagus in a pan of lightly salted boiling water for 3–5 minutes until just tender, drain and cool under cold running water.

Stir together the mustard, vinegar and cream, and then slowly whisk in the oil, a little at a time. Season well.

Arrange the asparagus on 4 plates and drizzle over the dressing. Shell and roughly chop the eggs, then scatter over the asparagus together with the capers and olives.

Broad Bean Bruschetta

SERVES 4
PREPARATION TIME 15 minutes
COOKING TIME 3 minutes

5 tablespoons extra virgin olive oil, plus extra for drizzling
2 garlic cloves (1 crushed and 1 left whole)
pinch of dried chilli flakes
handful of mint leaves

250 g (8 oz) shelled broad beans, thawed if frozen, skins removed
40 g (1½ oz) Pecorino, grated
1 small ciabatta loaf, cut into 8 thin slices
salt and pepper
Parmesan shavings, to serve

Combine the oil, crushed garlic, chillies and mint in a bowl and leave to infuse for 10 minutes.

Meanwhile, lightly crush the broad beans in a separate bowl with a fork. Season with salt and pepper, then toss into the oil mixture with the Pecorino. Toast the bread slices on both sides under a preheated medium grill or in a preheated ridged griddle pan.

Rub the toasted slices with the remaining garlic. Top with the broad bean mixture and drizzle over a little oil. Scatter with Parmesan shavings and serve immediately.

Olive, Onion & Rosemary Focaccia

SERVES 6
PREPARATION TIME 2 hours, 20 minutes
COOKING TIME about 20 minutes

15 g (½ oz) fresh yeast or
  1½ teaspoons fast-action
  dried yeast
large pinch of caster sugar
225 ml (7½ fl oz) lukewarm
  water
350 g (12 oz) Italian '00' flour
  or plain flour, plus extra
  for dusting

½ teaspoon salt
olive oil, for oiling and
  drizzling
1 onion, thinly sliced
50 g (2 oz) pitted black olives
3 rosemary sprigs, leaves only
coarse sea salt

Dissolve the yeast in a bowl with the sugar, measured water and half the flour. Cover with a moist cloth and leave to stand in a warm place for 15 minutes until foamy.

Stir the salt into the remaining flour, then tip into the yeast mixture. Stir with one hand to form a moist dough. Knead on a floured work surface for 10 minutes until smooth and elastic. It should be very soft and slightly sticky. If too sticky to handle, add a little more flour. Put in an oiled bowl, cover with a moist cloth and leave to rise in a warm place for 1 hour, or until doubled in size.

Gently knead half the onion and half the olives into the dough. Transfer to a lightly oiled rectangular baking tray, about 20 x 30 cm (8 x 12 inches), stretching it to fill the tray. Cover with a moist cloth and leave to rise in a warm place for 30 minutes. Make deep dimples on the surface with your finger. Scatter with the rosemary and remaining onion and olives and drizzle with oil. Cover again and leave to rise for 15 minutes.

Sprinkle the top of the focaccia with coarse sea salt. Bake in a preheated oven, 200°C (400°F), Gas Mark 6, for 20 minutes. The bread is ready when the base sounds hollow when tapped. If not, bake for a further 5 minutes. Turn out onto a wire rack and leave to cool. Eat warm or at room temperature on the same day.

Corn on the Cob with Turmeric Butter

SERVES 4
PREPARATION TIME 5 minutes
COOKING TIME 15–20 minutes

4 fresh or frozen corn on
  the cob
80 g (3 oz) unsalted butter
½ teaspoon grated fresh
  turmeric or ground
  turmeric

½ teaspoon ground cumin
sea salt and ground black
  pepper

Cook the corn on a hot griddle pan until soft and a
little charred.

Meanwhile, melt the butter in a small saucepan and
add the turmeric and cumin. Allow the spices to cook
in the butter for a few minutes for the flavours to infuse.

Serve the corn with the melted butter poured over
and season generously with salt and pepper.

Matcha & Red Lentil Hummus

SERVES 4
PREPARATION TIME 10 minutes
COOKING TIME 15 minutes + cooling

100 g (3½ oz) dried red lentils,
rinsed and drained
1 garlic clove, crushed
juice of ½ lemon, or to taste

1 tablespoon tahini
¼ teaspoon sea salt
¼ teaspoon matcha powder

Add the lentils to a saucepan, along with enough water to cover by 1 cm (½ inch). Bring to the boil, then reduce the heat and simmer for about 15 minutes, or until cooked and soft. Drain and set aside to cool.

Add the cooled lentils to a food processor or blender along with the remaining ingredients and blend to a soft, hummus-like consistency.

Taste and adjust the seasoning, adding more lemon juice if needed.

Yellow Rice with Coconut Halloumi

SERVES 2 (or 4 as a side)
PREPARATION TIME 10 minutes
COOKING TIME 10–20 minutes

zest of 1 lemon
1 teaspoon ground turmeric
1 teaspoon ground ginger
2 teaspoons yellow mustard
  seeds
150 g (5 oz) basmati rice,
  rinsed
300 ml (11 fl oz) hot vegetable
  stock)

8 kaffir lime leaves
100 g (3½ oz) halloumi, cubed
flour, for dusting
1 egg, beaten
50 g (2 oz) coconut flakes
vegetable oil, for frying
apple blossom flower or mint
  sprigs, to garnish

Dry-fry the lemon zest, turmeric, ginger and yellow mustard seeds in a saucepan until the seeds begin to pop. Add the rice, stock and kaffir lime leaves and bring to the boil. Reduce the heat and simmer for 10 minutes, or until the rice is fluffy and cooked and all the liquid has been absorbed.

Make the coconut halloumi. Dip the halloumi the cubes first into some flour, then the beaten egg, and finally the coconut flakes, pressing to coat on all sides.

Heat a shallow depth of vegetable oil in a wok and fry the coconut halloumi cubes until golden brown on all sides. Carefully remove with a slotted spoon and drain on kitchen paper. Set aside.

Fluff up the rice with a fork and top with the fried halloumi. Garnish with apple blossom or mint sprigs, if using, and serve immediately.

Summer Rolls with Matcha Dipping Sauce

MAKES 8 rolls

PREPARATION TIME 15 minutes + soaking

8 rice paper wrappers
large handful of anise hyssop
    leaves (or use 4 iceberg
    lettuce leaves, halved)
80 g (3 oz) pickled vegetables
200 g (7 oz) steamed salmon
    or sea bass, flaked
40 g (1½ oz) baby leaf spinach
40 g (1½ oz) coriander leaves

FOR THE DIPPING SAUCE

1 tablespoon coconut sugar
2 tablespoons lime juice
1 tablespoon fish sauce
½ teaspoon matcha powder
1 garlic clove, crushed
1 green chilli, thinly sliced
1 spring onion, thinly sliced

Fill a large bowl with warm water. Working in batches, soak 2 rice paper wrappers until softened, about 2 minutes. Remove the wrappers from the water and arrange in a single layer on your work surface.

Place a few anise hyssop leaves or half an iceberg leaf in the middle of each wrapper. Place a few strips of pickled vegetables in the middle, then a spoonful of steamed fish, then another few strips of pickled vegetables. Add a drizzle of the pickling liquid for flavour and top with a few baby spinach and coriander leaves.

Fold one edge of each wrapper over the filling. Fold in the ends, then roll up tightly, enclosing the filling. Transfer to a serving plate and repeat with the remaining wrappers and filling.

Make the dipping sauce. Whisk the sugar, lime juice and fish sauce together until dissolved, then whisk in the matcha powder before adding all the other ingredients. Serve in a bowl alongside the summer rolls.

Hot Potato Blinis with Beetroot

SERVES 4
PREPARATION TIME 15 minutes
COOKING TIME 10–15 minutes

200 g (7 oz) ready-made
  mashed potato
50 g (2 oz) self-raising flour
3 large eggs, separated
2 tablespoons soured cream
4 tablespoons finely chopped
  dill
vegetable oil, for frying
salt and pepper

FOR THE TOPPING
2 cooked beetroot, peeled
  and finely diced
6 tablespoons crème fraîche
1 tablespoon creamed
  horseradish
salt and pepper
chopped chives, to garnish

Place the mashed potato in a bowl. Beat in the flour, egg yolks, soured cream and dill and season well.

Whisk the egg whites in a large, grease-free bowl until stiff. Using a metal spoon, carefully fold the beaten egg whites into the potato mixture.

Heat a little oil in a large, nonstick frying pan. Add 3–4 separate tablespoons of the potato blini mixture. Fry over a medium heat until set, then turn the blinis over and fry briefly so that both sides are lightly browned. Remove and keep warm in a low oven. Repeat the process until all the potato mixture has been used.

Meanwhile, make the topping. Mix together most of the beetroot, reserving a little to garnish with the crème fraîche and creamed horseradish and season well.

Spoon the beetroot mixture over the blinis, garnish with the reserved beetroot, chopped chives and freshly ground black pepper.

Mains

Spicy Beef Burgers

SERVES 4
PREPARATION TIME 10 minutes
COOKING TIME 6–14 minutes

575 g (1 lb 3 oz) lean minced
   beef
2 garlic cloves, crushed
1 red onion, finely chopped
1 hot red chilli, finely chopped
bunch of parsley, chopped
1 tablespoon Worcestershire
   sauce
1 egg, beaten

4 wholemeal or granary rolls,
   split
hot salad leaves, such as
   mizuna or rocket
1 beefsteak tomato,
   sliced
salt and pepper
snipped chives, to garnish

Put the minced beef, garlic, onion, chilli and parsley in
a large bowl. Add the Worcestershire sauce, beaten egg
and a little salt and pepper and mix well.

Heat a griddle pan. Using your hands, divide the mixture
into 4 and shape into burgers. Cook the burgers in the
griddle pan for 3 minutes on each side for rare, 5 minutes
for medium or 7 minutes for well done.

Place the roll halves under a preheated hot grill and toast
on one side. Fill each bun with some hot salad leaves, some
tomato slices and a griddled burger. Garnish with snipped
chives and serve with your favourite relish.

Monkfish Kebabs

SERVES 4
PREPARATION TIME 10 minutes + marinating
COOKING TIME 8–10 minutes

1 kg (2 lb) monkfish fillet, cut
  into 4 cm (1½ inch) cubes
200 ml (7 fl oz) natural yogurt
4 tablespoons lemon juice
3 garlic cloves, crushed
2 teaspoons grated root
  ginger

1 teaspoon hot chilli powder
1 teaspoon ground cumin
1 teaspoon ground coriander
2 Thai red chillies, finely sliced
salt and pepper

Put the monkfish into a non-metallic bowl.

Mix together the yogurt, lemon juice, garlic, ginger, chilli powder, cumin, ground coriander and chillies in a small bowl, and season with salt and pepper. Pour this over the fish, cover and marinate in the refrigerator for 3–4 hours, or overnight if time allows.

Lift the fish out of the marinade and thread on to 8 flat metal skewers. Place on a grill rack and cook under a hot preheated grill for 8–10 minutes, turning once, until the fish is cooked through. Serve immediately, with a green salad and naan bread.

Garlic Mushroom & Chicken Pizza

SERVES 2
PREPARATION TIME 10 minutes
COOKING TIME 13 minutes

1 tablespoon sunflower
  oil
200 g (7 oz) mixed
  mushrooms, sliced
1 chopped ready-cooked
  chicken breast

1 large ready-made pizza base
2 tablespoons ready-made
  tomato sauce
125 g (4 oz) garlic and herb
  soft cheese
salt and pepper

Heat the oil in a large nonstick frying pan and fry the mushrooms for 3 minutes, then stir in the chicken, heat through and set aside.

Spread the pizza base with the tomato sauce, spoon the mushroom mixture over the top and dot with the soft cheese.

Bake in a preheated oven, 220°C (435°F) Gas Mark 7, for 10 minutes, or until the cheese is melted and the crust is golden.

Pasta Salad with Mozzarella & Asparagus

SERVES 4
PREPARATION TIME 10 minutes + marinating
COOKING TIME 4–5 minutes

500 g (1 lb) thin asparagus spears, trimmed
3–4 tablespoons extra virgin olive oil, plus extra to serve
juice of 1 lemon
400 g (13 oz) cooked penne
2 garlic cloves, roughly chopped
¼–½ teaspoon dried chilli flakes
25 g (1 oz) basil leaves
25 g (1 oz) grated Parmesan
200 g (7 oz) mozzarella, roughly chopped
salt and pepper

Brush the asparagus spears with a little of the oil. Cook in a preheated ridged griddle pan or under a preheated high grill, turning once, until charred and tender. Toss with a little more of the oil, half the lemon juice and salt and pepper.

Add the asparagus to a bowl of cooked pasta. Toss in the remaining ingredients, minus the mozzarella, and leave to marinate while the pasta and asparagus cool to room temperature.

Add the mozzarella and a drizzle of oil, before serving.

Antipasti & Pesto Pasta Salad

SERVES 4
PREPARATION TIME 10 minutes
COOKING TIME 8–12 minutes

300 g (10 oz) rigatoni or penne
50 g (2 oz) basil leaves
25 g (1 oz) toasted pine nuts
50 g (2 oz) Parmesa, grated
1 garlic clove, crushed
100 ml (3½ fl oz) olive oil
black pepper

300 g (10 oz) cherry tomatoes, halved
200 g (7 oz) mixed antipasti (artichokes, roasted peppers, mushrooms and aubergine), from a jar, drained
basil leaves, to serve

Cook the pasta according to the packet instructions.

Meanwhile, make the pesto by placing the basil, pine nuts, cheese, garlic and oil in a blender and whizz until fairly smooth.

Season with black pepper and place in a wide serving dish with the cherry tomatoes and mixed antipasti, then tip in the cooked pasta.

Toss to mix well, top with basil leaves and serve at room temperature.

Spaghetti with Charred Asparagus

SERVES 4
PREPARATION TIME 10 minutes
COOKING TIME 15 minutes

500 g (1 lb) thin asparagus spears, trimmed

3–4 tablespoons extra virgin olive oil

juice of 1 lemon

375 g (12 oz) dried spaghetti

2 garlic cloves, roughly chopped

¼–½ teaspoon dried chilli flakes

25 g (1 oz) basil leaves

25 g (1 oz) Parmesan, grated, plus extra to serve (optional)

salt and pepper

Brush the asparagus spears with a little of the oil. Cook in a preheated ridged griddle pan or under a preheated high grill, turning once, until charred and tender. Toss with a little more of the oil, half the lemon juice and salt and pepper. Set aside.

Cook the pasta in a large saucepan of salted boiling water for 8–10 minutes, or according to the packet instructions, until al dente.

Just before the pasta is cooked, heat the remaining oil in a large frying pan or wok over a medium heat. Add the garlic with a little salt and cook, stirring, for 3–4 minutes until softened but not browned. Add the chilli flakes and asparagus and heat through.

Drain the pasta, reserving a ladleful of the cooking water, and add both to the frying pan with the basil, remaining lemon juice, the Parmesan and pepper to taste. Serve immediately, with extra Parmesan, if liked.

Pea, Mint & Matcha Soup

SERVES 2
PREPARATION TIME 15 minutes
COOKING TIME 15 minutes

80 g (3 oz) chilled butter
1 leek, thinly sliced
2 garlic cloves, thinly sliced
1 medium waxy potato,
    peeled and diced
500 ml (18 fl oz) vegetable
    stock
250 g (8 oz) garden peas

2 teaspoons matcha powder,
    plus extra for dusting
15 g mint leaves
juice of ½ lime
2 teaspoons crème fraîche or
    natural yogurt
sea salt

Melt half the butter in a saucepan over a medium heat and fry the leek and garlic until softened. Add the potato and cook, stirring, for 2 minutes. Add the stock and a large pinch of salt and bring to a simmer.

Once the potatoes are cooked and offer little resistance to a knife, add the peas and matcha powder, bring back to a simmer and cook for another 2–3 minutes. Remove the pan from the heat, add the mint, reserving a few leaves to garnish, and set aside to infuse for about 2 minutes.

Reserve 2 ladles of cooking liquid, then blend the mixture using a hand-held blender. Dice the remaining chilled butter and whisk into the blended soup one cube at a time. If the mixture appears too thick – more like a purée than a soup – add some of the reserved liquid until the desired consistency has been reached.

Pass the blended soup though a fine sieve and stir in the lime juice. Garnish with a teaspoon of crème fraîche or yogurt and a few mint leaves.

Barley, Bean & Porcini Soup

SERVES 4
PREPARATION TIME 10 minutes + soaking
COOKING TIME 1 hour 35 minutes

100 g (3½ oz) dried borlotti
  beans
100 g (3½ oz) dried cannellini
  beans
2 litres (3½ pints) vegetable or
  chicken stock
2 celery sticks, diced
1 large carrot, diced
1 onion, diced
1 bay leaf
¼ teaspoon dried chilli flakes

75 g (3 oz) pearl barley
20 g (¾ oz) dried porcini
  mushrooms
2 tablespoons roughly
  chopped flat-leaf parsley
salt and pepper

TO SERVE
grated Parmesan
extra virgin olive oil

Put the dried beans in a large bowl, cover with cold water and leave to soak overnight.

Drain the soaked beans, put in a large saucepan and cover with the stock. Stir in the vegetables, bay leaf and chillies and bring to the boil. Reduce the heat and skim off any scum that has risen to the surface. Simmer, uncovered, for 1 hour.

Stir the pearl barley and porcini into the pan and quickly return to the boil. Skim off any scum, reduce the heat and simmer for a further 30 minutes, or until the beans and barley are very tender.

Add the parsley, then check the seasoning, adding salt and pepper to taste. Serve with a scattering of grated Parmesan and a light drizzle of oil.

Summer Vegetable Soup

SERVES 4
PREPARATION TIME 15 minutes
COOKING TIME about 25 minutes

1 teaspoon olive oil
1 leek, finely sliced
1 large potato, peeled and
    chopped
900 ml (1½ pints) vegetable
    stock

450 g (14½ oz) mixed summer
    vegetables (such as peas,
    asparagus, broad beans
    and courgettes)
2 tablespoons chopped mint
2 tablespoons crème fraîche
salt and pepper

Heat the oil in a medium saucepan and fry the leek for 3–4 minutes until softened.

Add the potato and stock to the pan and cook for 10 minutes. Add all the summer vegetables and the mint, then bring to the boil. Reduce the heat and simmer for 10 minutes.

Transfer the soup to a blender or food processor and purée until smooth. Return the soup to the pan, add the crème fraîche and season to taste with salt and pepper. Heat through gently and serve.

Summer
Green Pea Soup

SERVES 4
PREPARATION TIME 10 minutes
COOKING TIME about 15 minutes

1 tablespoon butter
bunch of spring onions,
  chopped
1.25 kg (2½ lb) fresh peas,
  shelled, or 500 g (1 lb) frozen
  peas
750 ml (1¼ pints) vegetable
  stock

2 tablespoons thick natural
  yogurt or single cream
nutmeg
1 tablespoon chopped chives,
  to garnish

Melt the butter in a large saucepan and soften the onions,
but do not allow them to colour. Add the peas to the pan
with the stock. Bring to the boil and simmer for 5 minutes
for frozen peas, but for up to 15 minutes for fresh peas, until
they are cooked. Be careful not to overcook fresh peas or
they will lose their flavour.

Remove from the heat and purée in a blender or food
processor. Add the yogurt or cream and grate in a little
nutmeg. Reheat gently if necessary, and serve sprinkled
with chives.

Prawn & Avocado Tostada

SERVES 4
PREPARATION TIME 10 minutes
COOKING TIME 4–5 minutes

4 large soft flour tortillas
1 small iceberg lettuce, shredded
300 g (10 oz) cooked peeled prawns
1 large, ripe but firm avocado, stoned, peeled and diced
2 tablespoons chopped coriander
1 tablespoon lime juice
salt and cracked black pepper
lime wedges, to serve

Heat a griddle pan and toast a tortilla for 30–60 seconds on each side until lightly charred. Immediately push it into a small, deep bowl and set aside. Repeat with the remaining tortillas to make 4 bowl-shaped tortillas. Place one-quarter of the lettuce inside each one.

Meanwhile, toss together the prawns, avocado, coriander and lime juice, and season to taste.

Divide the prawn and avocado mixture between the tortillas and serve with lime wedges for squeezing over.

Grilled Sea Bass with Salsa Verde

SERVES 4
PREPARATION TIME 10 minutes
COOKING TIME 12 minutes

olive oil, for rubbing
4 sea bass fillets
(about 150 g / 5 oz each)
salt and pepper

FOR THE SALSA VERDE
3 tablespoons olive oil
large handful of flat-leaf
parsley
small handful of basil
1 garlic clove, crushed
juice of ½ lemon
1 tablespoon capers, drained

Rub a little olive oil over the fish fillets and season with salt and pepper.

Heat a griddle pan until smoking hot, add the fish fillets, skin-side down, and cook for 7 minutes until the skin is crisp and golden. Turn the fish over and cook for a further 5 minutes until just cooked through.

Meanwhile, make the salsa verde. Put all the ingredients in a small food processor and whizz to a rough paste.

Place the fish on serving plates and spoon over the salsa verde. Serve with boiled new potatoes and a green salad.

Octopus with Garlic Dressing

SERVES 6–8
PREPARATION TIME 10 minutes + cooling
and marinating
COOKING TIME 1½ hours

1 onion, cut into wedges
1 teaspoon whole cloves
1 tablespoon salt
2 litres (3½ pints) water
500 g (1 lb) cleaned octopus,
bought at least 2 days
before cooking, and placed
in the freezer for 48 hours
to tenderize the meat

FOR THE MARINADE
6 tablespoons extra virgin
olive oil
2 garlic cloves, crushed
4 tablespoons chopped
parsley
1 teaspoon white wine
vinegar
salt and pepper

Put the onion, cloves and salt in a large saucepan, then add the measurement water and bring to the boil. Using tongs, dip the octopus in and out of the water about 4 times, returning the water to the boil before re-dipping, then immerse the octopus completely in the water. (This helps to make the flesh tender.) If there are several pieces of octopus, dip them 1 at a time.

Reduce the heat and cook the octopus very gently for 1 hour, then check to see whether it is tender. Cook for a further 15–30 minutes if necessary. Leave it to cool in the liquid, then drain, cut into bite-sized pieces and place in a non-metallic bowl.

Make the marinade. Mix all the ingredients in a small bowl, season with salt and pepper and add to the bowl with the octopus. Mix well, cover and leave to marinate in the refrigerator for several hours or overnight. Serve the octopus with bread for mopping up the juices.

Swordfish with Salsa Verde

SERVES 4
PREPARATION TIME 20 minutes
COOKING TIME 4–6 minutes

1½ teaspoons Dijon mustard
450 ml (¾ pint) extra virgin
    olive oil
4 anchovy fillets in oil,
    drained and chopped
handful each of parsley, basil,
    mint and tarragon

2 tablespoons drained capers
1 garlic clove, crushed
2 tablespoons olive oil
4 swordfish steaks
    (about 150 g / 5 oz each)
juice of 1 lemon
salt and pepper

Whisk together the mustard and 250 ml (8 fl oz) of the oil in a bowl until they have emulsified. Stir in the anchovies.

Finely chop the herbs and capers together, then add these to the oil mixture along with the garlic. Gradually add more of the oil until the salsa has a spooning consistency.

Heat a griddle pan until hot. Brush the swordfish steaks on both sides with a little oil and season well. Griddle the steaks for 2–3 minutes on each side, or until cooked through but still very moist.

Add the lemon juice to the salsa verde, stir and spoon over the griddled fish. Serve immediately with a crisp green salad.

Summer Prawn & Fish Filo Pie

SERVES 4
PREPARATION TIME 10 minutes
COOKING TIME 20–25 minutes

750 g (1½ lb) skinless white fish fillets
100 g (3½ oz) frozen cooked peeled prawns, defrosted
100 g (3½ oz) frozen peas, defrosted
grated rind and juice of 1 lemon
600 ml (1 pint) ready-made white sauce
bunch of dill, chopped
8 sheets of filo pastry
melted butter, for brushing
salt and pepper

Cut the fish into large, bite-sized pieces and put in a bowl with the prawns and peas. Add the lemon rind and juice, stir in the white sauce and dill and season well with salt and pepper.

Tip the fish mixture into a gratin or pie dish. Cover the surface with the sheets of filo pastry, scrunching up each sheet into a loosely crumpled ball. Brush the pastry with melted butter.

Bake in a preheated oven, 200°C (400°F), Gas Mark 6, for 20–25 minutes until the pastry is golden brown and the fish is cooked through.

Tuscan-Style Tarts

SERVES 4
PREPARATION TIME 15 minutes
COOKING TIME 12–15 minutes

375 g (12 oz) ready-rolled puff
pastry, defrosted if frozen
2 tomatoes, sliced
150 g (5 oz) ready-cooked
chicken, sliced
8 small pieces of ready-
roasted red pepper, from
a jar, drained

1 tablespoon thyme leaves
125 g (4 oz) Kalamata olives
1 tablespoon olive oil
salt and pepper

Unroll the ready-rolled puff pastry, cut it into 4 x 12 cm
(5 inch) circles and place, well spaced apart, on a large
baking sheet. Prick the bases all over with a fork.

Arrange the tomato slices randomly on top of each one,
dividing them evenly between the bases and keeping a
1 cm (½ inch) border around the edge. Evenly scatter over
the chicken, peppers, thyme and olives, then drizzle with
the olive oil and season to taste.

Bake at the top of a preheated oven, 220°C (425°F),
Gas Mark 7, for 12–15 minutes, or until the pastry is puffed
and golden and the topping soft. Serve the tarts with a
simple green salad.

Caramelized Onion & Anchovy Tart

SERVES 4
PREPARATION TIME 25 minutes + chilling
COOKING TIME 55 minutes– 1 hour

FOR THE PASTRY
200 g (7 oz) plain flour, plus
    extra for dusting
85 g (3¼ oz) chilled lightly
    salted butter, cubed
1 egg
1 egg yolk

FOR THE FILLING
25 g (1 oz) butter
2 tablespoons olive oil

3 large onions, finely sliced
2 thyme sprigs
2 eggs
100 ml (3½ fl oz) milk
100 ml (3½ fl oz) double cream
2 tomatoes, thinly sliced
8 anchovy fillets from a can,
    drained
salt and pepper

Make the pastry. Place all the pastry ingredients in a food processor and blend until they form a soft dough, adding a drop of cold water if necessary.

Knead lightly until smooth, then wrap in clingfilm and chill for at least 30 minutes.

Roll out the pastry on a lightly floured work surface until about 3 mm (⅛ inch) thick and use to line a 23 cm (9 inch) fluted tart tin. Trim off the excess pastry and chill for 1 hour.

Line the tart with baking paper and fill with baking beans. Bake in a preheated oven, 180°C (350°F), Gas Mark 4, for 10–12 minutes until lightly golden. Remove the baking paper and beans, then return to the oven and cook for a further 2 minutes to dry out the base. Remove from the oven and leave to cool, leaving the oven on.

Make the filling. Heat the butter and oil in a frying pan, add the onions and thyme and fry over a low heat for about 20 minutes until the onions are golden brown.

Remove the thyme and spread the onions over the tart base. Whisk together the eggs, milk and cream in a bowl, season with salt and pepper and pour over the onions.

Bake in the oven for 10 minutes until slightly risen and starting to set. Arrange the tomatoes and anchovies on top of the tart, then return to the oven and cook for a further 10–15 minutes until the filling has set completely. Leave to cool for 5 minutes before serving

Salmon & Asparagus En Croûte

SERVES 4
PREPARATION TIME 25 minutes
COOKING TIME 40–45 minutes

25 g (1 oz) butter
175 g (6 oz) asparagus, trimmed
600–625 g (1 lb 2 oz–1 lb 4 oz) salmon fillet, about 18–20 cm (7–8 inches) long, skinned
juice of ½ lemon
500 g (1 lb) ready-made puff pastry, defrosted if frozen
flour, for dusting
100 g (3½ oz) soft cheese
grated rind of 1 lemon

1 tablespoon chopped tarragon
2 tablespoons chopped parsley
1½ teaspoons green peppercorns, drained and chopped (optional)
50 g (2 oz) sunblush tomatoes, drained and roughly chopped
beaten egg, to glaze
salt flakes, for sprinkling (optional)
salt and pepper

Heat the butter in a frying pan, add the asparagus and fry for 2–3 minutes until just softened, then season with salt and pepper. Drizzle the salmon with lemon juice and season.

Roll the pastry out thinly on a lightly floured surface and trim to a 35 cm (14 inch) square, then trim a 3.5 cm (1½ inch) strip off one of the sides. Place the salmon on top so that the long side of the salmon is parallel with the shorter side of the pastry rectangle.

Dot the cheese on top of the salmon, then sprinkle with the lemon rind, herbs, peppercorns if using, and tomatoes. Arrange the asparagus on top, alternating their direction.

Brush the pastry around the salmon with beaten egg, then fold the narrower sides up and over the salmon, pressing to seal. Cut the excess from the top ends of pastry, then fold and press to wrap the salmon like a parcel.

Brush the parcel with beaten egg and transfer to a baking sheet. Decorate, and sprinkle with salt flakes, if liked.

Bake in a preheated oven, 200°C (400°F), Gas Mark 6, for 35–40 minutes. Check after 25 minutes and cover with foil if the pastry seems to be browning too quickly. To test if the salmon is cooked, insert a knife into the centre, wait 3 seconds, then remove; if the knife feels hot it is cooked. Cut into thick slices and serve with lemon wedges.

Torta Pasqualina

SERVES 6
PREPARATION TIME 30 minutes + chilling
COOKING TIME 45–50 minutes

375 g (12 oz) ready-rolled
   shortcrust pastry
flour, for dusting
butter, for greasing
175 g (6 oz) chargrilled
   artichokes in olive oil
1 onion, chopped
2 garlic cloves, finely chopped
250 g (8 oz) spinach, rinsed
and drained
175 g (6 oz) cherry tomatoes,
   halved
75 g (3 oz) Parmesan, grated
4 eggs
250 ml (8 fl oz) milk
salt and pepper

Roll the pastry out thinly on a lightly floured surface until a little larger than a 28 × 20 cm (11 × 8 inch) fluted loose-bottomed rectangular tart tin. Grease the tin with butter.

Lift the pastry over a rolling pin, drape into the tin, then press over the base and sides. Trim off the excess pastry with scissors so that it stands a little above the top of the tin. Chill for 15 minutes.

Drain off 1 tablespoon oil from the artichokes into a frying pan, add the onion and garlic and fry for 5 minutes until softened. Scoop out of the pan and reserve. Add the spinach to the pan and fry for 2–3 minutes until just wilted. Tip into a sieve and press out the juices.

Put the tart tin on a baking sheet. Arrange the spinach in the base of the pastry case, drain and arrange the artichoke hearts and halved tomatoes on top, then sprinkle with the Parmesan. Beat the eggs and milk with a little salt and pepper and pour into the tart.

Bake in a preheated oven, 190°C (375°F), Gas Mark 5, for 30–40 minutes until golden brown and the filling is just set. Leave to cool for 15 minutes, then remove the tart from the tin. Cut into squares and serve warm or cold.

Italian Goats' Cheese Tart

SERVES 6
PREPARATION TIME 30 minutes + chilling
COOKING TIME 45–50 minutes

375 g (12 oz) ready-rolled shortcrust pastry

flour, for dusting

butter, for greasing

1 tablespoon olive oil

1 onion, chopped

2 garlic cloves, finely chopped

250 g (8 oz) spinach, rinsed, drained

100 g (3½ oz) goats' cheese, diced

175 g (6 oz) cherry tomatoes, halved

75 g (3 oz) Parmesan, grated

4 eggs

250 ml (8 fl oz) milk

salt and pepper

Roll the pastry out thinly on a lightly floured surface until a little larger than a 28 × 20 cm (11 × 8 inch) fluted loose-bottomed rectangular tart tin. Grease the tin with butter.

Lift the pastry over a rolling pin, drape into the tin, then press over the base and sides. Trim off the excess pastry with scissors so that it stands a little above the top of the tin. Chill for 15 minutes.

Heat the oil in a frying pan, add the onion and garlic and fry for 5 minutes until softened. Scoop out of the pan and reserve. Add the spinach to the pan and fry for 2–3 minutes until just wilted. Tip into a sieve and press out the juices.

Put the tart tin on a baking sheet. Arrange the spinach in the base of the pastry case, drain and arrange the goats' cheese and halved tomatoes on top, then sprinkle with the Parmesan. Beat the eggs and milk with a little salt and pepper and pour into the tart.

Bake in a preheated oven, 190°C (375°F), Gas Mark 5, for 30–40 minutes until golden brown and the filling is just set. Leave to cool for 15 minutes, then remove the tart from the tin. Cut into squares and serve warm or cold.

Mixed Seafood Puff Pies

MAKES 4
PREPARATION TIME 30 minutes
COOKING TIME 40–45 minutes

300 g (10 oz) white fish fillets, such as cod or haddock
300 g (10 oz) salmon fillet, cut into 2 pieces
600 ml (1 pint) milk
2 bay leaves
rind of 1 lemon, pared into strips with a vegetable peeler
50 g (2 oz) butter
50 g (2 oz) plain flour, plus extra for dusting
150 ml (¼ pint) fish stock

125 g (4 oz) sweetcorn
bunch of spring onions, finely sliced
100 g (3½ oz) Cheddar, grated
400 g (13 oz) frozen mixed seafood, defrosted, rinsed with cold water and drained
500 g (1 lb) ready-made puff pastry, defrosted if frozen
beaten egg, to glaze
salt and pepper

Lay the fish fillets in a frying pan, pour over just enough of the milk to cover, then add the bay leaves, lemon rind and salt and pepper. Cover and simmer for 8, minutes or until the fish is just cooked and flakes easily.

Lift the fish out onto a plate, peel away the skin, then break into large flakes, removing any bones. Strain the milk and mix with the remaining milk.

Heat the butter in a saucepan, stir in the flour and cook briefly, then gradually mix in the milk and bring to the boil, stirring. Stir in the fish stock and cook over a low heat for 3–4 minutes. Stir in the sweetcorn, spring onions and cheese, then season generously with salt and pepper. Cover the surface of the sauce with wetted greaseproof or nonstick paper and leave to cool.

Fold the flaked fish and mixed seafood into the sauce, then spoon into 4 individual round pie dishes. Roll the pastry out thinly on a lightly floured surface and cut out 4 pastry lids. Brush the dish rims with beaten egg and press the lids in place. Cut fish shapes from the pastry trimmings and arrange on top, then glaze with beaten egg.

Bake in a preheated oven, 200°C (400°F), Gas Mark 6, for 25–30 minutes until the pastry is well risen and golden and the filling is piping hot.

Spinach, Tomato & Egg Tarts

SERVES 6
PREPARATION TIME 10 minutes
COOKING TIME 20 minutes

3 tablespoons olive oil
3 garlic cloves, finely chopped
½ teaspoon hot smoked
  paprika
200 g (7 oz) can chopped
  tomatoes
200 g (7 oz) baby spinach
  leaves

6 ready-made savoury tart
  cases, each 8 cm (3¼ inch)
  in diameter
6 eggs
100 g (3½ oz) Manchego,
  grated
salt and pepper

Heat half the oil in a saucepan, add the garlic and cook for 30 seconds, then stir in the paprika. Add the tomatoes and a little water if necessary and simmer for 10 minutes until most of the liquid has evaporated and the mixture has thickened, then season.

Place the spinach in a large colander and pour over boiling water until wilted. Leave to cool slightly, then squeeze out any excess water and roughly chop.

Arrange the tart cases on a baking sheet. Divide the spinach between the pastry cases, then spoon a little of the tomato sauce over each one. Break 1 egg on top of each, sprinkle with the cheese and then drizzle over the remaining oil. Bake in a preheated oven, 200°C (400°F), Gas Mark 6, for 10 minutes, or until the eggs are cooked to your liking.

Veg-Forward

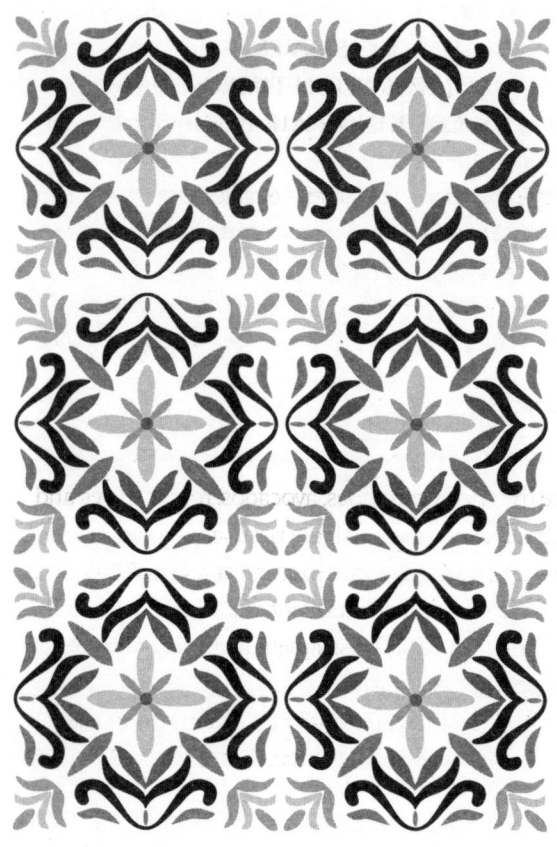

Cherry Tomato, Avocado & Mozzarella Pasta

SERVES 4
PREPARATION TIME 15 minutes
COOKING TIME 8–10 minutes

300 g (10 oz) cherry tomatoes, finely chopped
2 avocados, peeled, stoned and chopped
50 g (2 oz) rocket leaves
200 g (7 oz) mozzarella, chopped

6 tablespoons ready-made fresh green pesto
2 tablespoons olive oil
375 g (12 oz) dried spaghetti
salt and pepper

Place the cherry tomatoes, avocados, rocket leaves and mozzarella in a bowl with the pesto and olive oil. Season and stir to mix well. Leave to stand at room temperature for 15 minutes for the flavours to infuse.

Meanwhile, cook the spaghetti according to the packet instructions until al dente.

Drain the pasta and transfer to a wide serving dish. Add the cherry tomato mixture, toss to mix well and serve.

Asparagus Linguine with Lemon Carbonara Sauce

SERVES 4
PREPARATION TIME 5 minutes
COOKING TIME 10–12 minutes

400 g (13 oz) dried linguine
bunch of asparagus spears,
   trimmed
1 egg

3 tablespoons crème fraîche
juice of 1 small lemon
salt and pepper
Parmesan shavings, to serve

Cook the pasta according to the packet instructions until al dente. Add the asparagus 3 minutes before the end of the cooking time and cook until just tender.

Meanwhile, mix together the egg, crème fraîche and a good squeeze of lemon juice in a bowl.

Drain the pasta and asparagus and return to the pan. Toss through the egg sauce and serve immediately scattered with Parmesan shavings.

Creamy Asparagus Cappellacci

SERVES 4
PREPARATION TIME 10 minutes
COOKING TIME 15–20 minutes

400 g (13 oz) cappellacci
bunch of asparagus spears,
    trimmed
15 g (½ oz) butter
1 garlic clove, sliced

150 g (5 oz) mixed wild
    mushrooms, trimmed and
    halved if large
75 g (3 oz) crème fraîche
salt and pepper
Parmesan shavings, to serve

Cook the pasta according to the packet instructions until al dente. Add the asparagus 3 minutes before the end of the cooking time and cook until just tender.

Meanwhile, heat the butter in a frying pan, add the garlic and cook for 1 minute, then stir in the mushrooms and cook for 5 minutes until soft and golden. Stir in the crème fraîche.

Drain the pasta and asparagus, reserving a little of the cooking water, and return to the pan. Stir through the mushroom sauce and season, adding a little cooking water to loosen if needed. Spoon into serving bowls and serve scattered with Parmesan shavings.

Pea & Mint Risotto

SERVES 4
PREPARATION TIME 10 minutes
COOKING TIME 30 minutes

1 tablespoon olive oil
2 shallots, finely diced
400 g (13 oz) arborio risotto
   rice
100 ml (3½ fl oz) white wine
about 900 ml (1½ pints) hot
   vegetable stock

100 g (3½ oz) fresh or frozen
   peas, defrosted
small handful of mint leaves,
   chopped
40 g (1½ oz) butter
40 g (1½ oz) Parmesan, grated
salt and pepper

Heat the oil in a large saucepan and sauté the shallots for
2–3 minutes until softened.

Stir in the rice and cook, stirring, until the edges of the
grains look translucent. Pour in the wine and cook for
1–2 minutes until it is absorbed.

Add a ladleful of the hot vegetable stock and cook,
stirring continuously, until it has all been absorbed. Repeat
with the remaining hot stock, adding a ladleful at a time,
until the rice is al dente.

Stir in the peas, mint, butter and half the Parmesan,
season with salt and pepper and cook for 2–3 minutes.

Serve sprinkled with the remaining Parmesan.

Sweet Potato 'Bruschetta'

SERVES 2–4
PREPARATION TIME 10 minutes
COOKING TIME 20–25 minutes

2 sweet potatoes
(about 400 g / 13 oz), cut
into 5 mm (¼ inch) discs
4 tablespoons olive oil
200 g (7 oz) tomatoes,
roughly chopped
½ small red onion, finely
chopped

1 tablespoon balsamic vinegar
or red wine vinegar
large handful of basil leaves,
roughly chopped
½ garlic clove
salt and pepper

Toss the potatoes with 2 tablespoons of the oil. Spread out in a single layer on a baking tray. Bake in a preheated oven, 200°C (400°F), Gas Mark 6, for 20–25 minutes.

In a bowl, toss the tomatoes, remaining olive oil, onion and vinegar and season to taste. Stir through half the basil.

When the sweet potatoes are done, rub one side of the surface with the cut side of the garlic clove, then top with the tomato mixture, sprinkling with the reserved basil.

Eat immediately.

Creamy Asparagus Puff Pie

SERVES 6
PREPARATION TIME 25 minutes
COOKING TIME 30–40 minutes

500 g (1 lb) ready-made puff
    pastry, defrosted if frozen
flour, for dusting
beaten egg, to glaze
250 g (8 oz) bunch of
    asparagus
1 bunch of spring onions
1 tablespoon olive oil

125 g (4 oz) mascarpone
1 large garlic clove, finely
    chopped
25 g (1 oz) Parmesan, grated,
    plus extra for sprinkling
salt and pepper

Roll out the pastry thickly on a lightly floured surface and trim to a 23 × 30 cm (9 × 12 inch) rectangle. Transfer to an oiled baking sheet and use a little beaten egg to glaze. Lightly score a line 2.5 cm (1 inch) in from the edges, then prick the inside rectangle with a fork.

Bake in a preheated oven, 200°C (400°F), Gas Mark 6, for 10 minutes. Press down the centre with the back of a fork, then bake for 5–10 minutes more until the pastry is cooked through. Press down the centre once more.

Meanwhile, trim 2.5 cm (1 inch) from the base of the asparagus, then trim the spring onions to the same length. Toss the asparagus and spring onions in the oil and plenty of salt and pepper, then cook on a preheated ridged frying pan for 5 minutes, turning, until just cooked.

Beat the mascarpone with the garlic, Parmesan, remaining beaten egg and salt and pepper. Spoon into the centre of the pie case and spread into an even layer. Arrange the asparagus and spring onions alternately on top and sprinkle with a little extra Parmesan.

Bake for 10–15 minutes until the filling is just set. Check after 10 minutes and cover with kitchen foil if the pastry seems to be browning too quickly.

Goats' Cheese & Beetroot Tart

SERVES 6
PREPARATION TIME 30 minutes + chilling
COOKING TIME 45–50 minutes

375 g (12 oz) ready-rolled
   shortcrust pastry
flour, for dusting
butter, for greasing
1 tablespoon olive oil
1 onion, chopped
200 g (7 oz) raw, trimmed
   beetroot, coarsely grated

4 eggs
250 ml (8 fl oz) milk
1 teaspoon Dijon mustard
small bunch of thyme
150 g (5 oz) goats' cheese log
salt and cayenne pepper

Roll the pastry out on a lightly floured surface until a little larger than a 24 cm (9½ inch) fluted loose-bottomed tart tin. Grease the tin with butter. Lift the pastry over a rolling pin, drape into the tin, then press over the base and sides. Trim off the excess pastry with scissors so that it stands a little above the top of the tin. Chill for 15 minutes.

Meanwhile, heat the oil in a frying pan, add the onion and fry until softened. Add the beetroot and cook for 2–3 minutes. Beat the eggs, milk and mustard together in a bowl. Add the onion, some of the thyme leaves torn from the stems and a generous amount of salt and cayenne pepper. Leave to stand for 5 minutes.

Put the tart tin on a baking sheet and pour the beetroot mixture into the tart case. Cut the cheese into 6 thick slices, arrange in a ring on top of the tart and sprinkle with the remaining thyme leaves and a little salt and cayenne pepper.

Bake in a preheated oven, 180°C (350°F), Gas Mark 4, for 40–45 minutes until the filling is set. Leave to cool for at least 15 minutes, then remove the tin and transfer the tart to a plate. Serve warm or cold, cut into wedges, with a green salad.

Wild Mushroom Tart

SERVES 4
PREPARATION TIME 15 minutes
COOKING TIME 25 minutes

375 g (12 oz) ready-rolled
  shortcrust pastry
2 tablespoons olive oil
1 red onion, sliced
350 g (12 oz) mixed wild and
  chestnut mushrooms,
  trimmed and sliced

2 eggs, beaten
100 g (3½ oz) mascarpone
1 teaspoon thyme leaves
2 teaspoons wholegrain
  mustard
40 g (1½ oz) Parmesan, grated
pepper

Use the pastry to line a 23 cm (9 inch) flan tin. Chill while you make the filling.

Heat the oil in a frying pan and cook the onion and mushrooms for 5 minutes, stirring frequently.

Meanwhile, beat together the eggs, mascarpone and thyme leaves in a bowl and season with pepper. Add the onion and mushrooms to the egg mixture and mix well.

Spread the mustard over the flan base. Pour over the filling and level with the back of a spoon.

Sprinkle with the Parmesan. Bake in a preheated oven, 200°C (400°F), Gas Mark 6, for 20 minutes until golden. Slice into generous pieces and serve hot or cold.

Pitta Pizzas with Sun-Dried Tomatoes

MAKES 3
PREPARATION TIME 10 minutes
COOKING TIME 10 minutes

200 g (7 oz) jar of sun-dried tomatoes, drained
3 pitta breads
½ garlic clove, sliced
1 teaspoon dried oregano
2 tablespoons vegan 'Parmesan'
100 g (3½ oz) cherry tomatoes, halved

½ green pepper, finely sliced
50 g (2 oz) black olives, halved
salt and pepper

TO SERVE
small handful of basil leaves (optional)
1 tablespoon olive oil

Blitz the sun-dried tomatoes in a food processor or with a stick blender until you have a smooth paste.

Lay the pitta breads on a baking tray. Spread 1 tablespoon of the sun-dried tomato purée on each pitta, followed by garlic slices and a little of oregano and vegan 'Parmesan'. Top with the tomatoes, green peppers and olives.

Bake in a preheated the oven, 220°C (425°F), Gas Mark 7, for 10 minutes. Remove from the oven, season and eat immediately, sprinkled with basil, if using, and oil.

Lettuce, Pea & Tarragon Soup

SERVES 4
PREPARATION TIME 10 minutes
COOKING TIME 10 minutes

2 tablespoons butter
8 spring onions, trimmed
  and sliced
750 g (1½ lb) frozen peas
1 tablespoon chopped
  tarragon leaves
1 cos lettuce, finely shredded

1 litre (1¾ pints) hot vegetable
  stock
salt and pepper

TO SERVE
2 tablespoons double cream
tarragon sprigs, to garnish
  (optional)

Melt the butter in a large saucepan over a medium heat. Add the spring onions and cook, stirring continuously, for 2 minutes. Stir in the peas, half the tarragon and the lettuce. Cook for 1 minute.

Add the stock, bring to the boil, cover and simmer for 5 minutes, or until the lettuce is tender.

Pour the soup into a blender, add the remaining tarragon and whizz until smooth. Season to taste.

Ladle into bowls, swirl over the cream and season with black pepper. Garnish with tarragon sprigs, if liked.

Spanish Almond & Onion Soup

SERVES 4–6
PREPARATION TIME 10 minutes
COOKING TIME 45–50 minutes

1 tablespoon olive oil
15 g (2 oz) butter
5 onions, sliced
1 garlic clove, sliced
25 g (1 oz) ground almonds
pinch of sweet paprika

50 ml (2 fl oz) sherry
900 ml (1½ pints) hot
   vegetable stock
Manchego, grated to serve
salt and pepper

Heat the oil and butter in a frying pan, add the onions and cook over a low heat for 20–25 minutes until very soft.

Add the garlic and cook for a further 2 minutes.

Stir in the ground almonds and paprika and cook for 3 minutes, then pour in the sherry and leave to bubble away. Pour in the hot vegetable stock and simmer for 20 minutes.

Ladle into bowls and serve sprinkled with Manchego.

Roasted Cauliflower Soup with Crunchy Leaf Croutons

SERVES 4
PREPARATION TIME 10 minutes
COOKING TIME 35–40 minutes

1 cauliflower, cut into small
   florets, leaves reserved
4 tablespoons olive oil
1 onion, roughly chopped
leaves from 2 thyme sprigs
4 garlic cloves, finely grated

1.5 litres (2½ pints) vegetable
   stock
juice of ½ lemon
salt and pepper

Place the cauliflower florets on a baking tray and toss with 2 tablespoons of the oil. Season well. Roast in a preheated oven, 200°C (400°F), Gas Mark 6, for 20 minutes.

Meanwhile, cook the onion in a large saucepan in 1 tablespoon of the oil for about 5 minutes until soft and translucent. Add the thyme leaves and garlic and cook for 1 minute. Pour in the stock and bring to a simmer.

When the cauliflower florets are browned, toss the cauliflower leaves with the remaining 1 tablespoon oil, season and roast for 5–10 minutes until crisp. Meanwhile, add the florets to the pan of stock and cook for 5 minutes.

Use a stick blender to whizz the soup until smooth. Season to taste with lemon juice and salt, then serve with the crispy leaf croutons.

Carrot, Beetroot & Orange Salad

SERVES 4
PREPARATION TIME 15 minutes

250 g (8 oz) carrots, peeled
250 g (8 oz) beetroot, peeled
2 oranges
2 teaspoons cumin seeds
1 teaspoon caraway seeds
2 tablespoons olive oil
finely grated zest and juice
of 1 lemon
small handful of mint leaves,
roughly chopped
small handful of dill, roughly
chopped
salt and pepper

Shred the carrots and beetroot. Use a small serrated knife to remove the peel and pith from the oranges, then slice into rounds and then half moons.

Toss the vegetables and oranges in a large salad bowl with the spices, oil, lemon zest and juice and herbs. Season well and serve.

Rice Noodle Salad

SERVES 4
PREPARATION TIME 20 minutes + soaking

150 g (5 oz) rice noodles
2 spring onions, finely sliced
1 carrot, grated or julienned
½ cucumber, grated
½ white cabbage, shredded
small handful of coriander
    and mint leaves, roughly
    chopped, plus extra
    (optional) to serve

FOR THE DRESSING
1 garlic clove, finely grated
4 tablespoons soy sauce
2 tablespoons lime juice
1 tablespoon light brown
    sugar
1 tablespoon sesame oil
2 tablespoons crispy chilli oil
salt

TO SERVE
2 tablespoons salted roasted
    peanuts, roughly chopped
½ red pepper, finely sliced

Cover the rice noodles with boiling water and set aside.

Put all the vegetables and herbs in a large bowl.

Make the dressing. Mix together all the ingredients in a
separate bowl, season to taste, then pour over the vegetables.

Drain the rice noodles once tender and add to the bowl,
tossing well to combine.

Serve sprinkled with extra herbs, if liked, the peanuts
and red pepper.

Sweet Potato Bulgur

SERVES 2
PREPARATION TIME 15 minutes
COOKING TIME 30–35 minutes

1 large sweet potato, peeled and roughly chopped

1½ teaspoons ground turmeric

1 teaspoon cumin seeds

2–3 tablespoons olive oil

100 g (3½ oz) bulgur wheat

1 teaspoon bouillon powder

100 g (3½ oz) baby spinach or baby kale, shredded

2 tablespoons extra virgin olive oil

zest and juice of ½ lime

50 ml (2 oz) baked kefir or natural yogurt

sea salt

coriander leaves, to serve

Mix the potato in a large bowl with 1 teaspoon of the ground turmeric, the cumin seeds, oil and a good pinch of salt. Transfer to a roasting tin. Roast in a preheated oven, 220°C (425°F), Gas Mark 7, for about 20 minutes until the sweet potato is soft and a little crispy at the edges. Turn halfway through cooking.

Place the bulgur wheat in a saucepan, cover with 1 litre (1¾ pints) of water, then add the bouillon and remaining ground turmeric. Bring to the boil, then reduce the heat and simmer for 10–12 minutes until cooked. Drain.

Toss the bulgur and roasted sweet potato together with the spinach or kale and the oil in a large bowl. Transfer to a salad platter.

Mix the lime zest and juice into the kefir or yogurt and drizzle over the salad. Scatter over the coriander leaves. Serve warm, or leave to cool, then chill in the refrigerator until needed.

Salsa Verde Sweet Potatoes

SERVES 4
PREPARATION TIME 20 minutes
COOKING TIME 25 minutes

4 sweet potatoes
2 tablespoons olive oil
salt and pepper
Parmesan (optional),
   to serve

FOR THE SALSA VERDE
large handful of soft herb
   leaves, such as basil, mint,
   oregano or parsley, plus
   extra to serve
finely grated zest and juice
   of 1 lemon
1 tablespoon capers, drained
2 garlic cloves
2 teaspoons Dijon mustard
2 teaspoons red wine vinegar
50 ml (2 fl oz) olive oil

Hasselback the sweet potatoes by slicing them at 3 mm (⅛ inch) intervals along their length, but not all the way through, so the sweet potato stays connected.

Drizzle with the oil and season well. Roast in a preheated oven, 220°C (425°F), Gas Mark 7, for 25 minutes until tender.

Meanwhile, make the salsa verde. Whizz all the ingredients together in a blender. Season to taste – it should be sharp and lively.

Serve the baked sweet potatoes drizzled with plenty of salsa verde and showered in Parmesan and herbs, if you like.

Something Different

Smoked Duck Citrus Salad

SERVES 4

PREPARATION TIME 15 minutes

2 clementines
100 g (3½ oz) watercress
50 g (2 oz) walnuts,
    lightly crushed
200 g (7 oz) smoked duck
    breast, sliced

TO GARNISH (OPTIONAL)
cress leaves
pomegranate seeds

FOR THE DRESSING
2 tablespoons walnut oil
2 teaspoons raspberry
    vinegar
salt and pepper

Cut away the peel and pith from the clementines. Cut the flesh into segments, discarding the membrane, but reserving the juice in a small bowl.

Arrange the watercress on plates and sprinkle with the clementine segments and the walnuts. Top with the smoked duck slices and garnish with the cress leaves and pomegranate seeds, if liked.

Make the dressing. Whisk the oil and vinegar into the reserved clementine juice and season to taste. Drizzle over the salad and serve.

Salmon with Almond Butter Matcha Crumb

SERVES 2
PREPARATION TIME 10 minutes
COOKING TIME 5–6 minutes

2 thick salmon fillets
(about 130 g / 4½ oz each)
3 teaspoons wholegrain
mustard
2 tablespoons coarse
almond butter
30g (1 oz) pumpkin seeds,
lightly crushed
zest of 1 lime

⅔ teaspoon matcha powder
1 teaspoon olive oil
1 teaspoon honey
1 tablespoon vegetable oil
sea salt and ground black
pepper
lime juice, to serve

Season both sides of the salmon fillets with a light sprinkling of sea salt and set aside.

In the meantime, put 1 teaspoon of the wholegrain mustard into a bowl with the almond butter, pumpkin seeds, lime zest, matcha powder, olive oil and honey and mix thoroughly to make the crumb. Season with a pinch of salt and a generous grinding of pepper.

Pat the salmon fillets dry, then spread the flesh side with the remaining mustard. Spread the crumb evenly on top.

Heat the vegetable oil in an ovenproof frying pan over a medium–high heat. Add the salmon fillets, skin-side down, pressing them lightly until they have relaxed. Roast in a preheated oven, 240°C (475°F), Gas Mark 9, for 4–5 minutes until the green of the crumb is slightly browned and the fish is medium-rare.

Squeeze lime juice over the salmon before serving.

Halibut Ceviche with Grapefruit

SERVES 2
PREPARATION TIME 10–15 minutes + chilling

450 g (14½ oz) skinless
  halibut fillet
2 limes
1 grapefruit
100 g (3½ oz) cherry tomatoes,
  halved

1 red chilli, deseeded
  (optional) and sliced
handful of mint, finely sliced
1 tablespoon extra virgin
  olive oil
salt and pepper

Using a very sharp knife, cut the fish into thin slices.

Grate the rind from 1 lime into a non-metallic bowl, then squeeze in the juice from both limes. Cut off the base of the grapefruit, then cut around the flesh to remove the rind and pith. Slice into segments and set aside. Add any juice from the grapefruit to the bowl.

Add the fish to the lime and grapefruit juices and toss to coat. Cover and leave to marinate in the refrigerator for 15 minutes.

Discard the marinade from the fish. Arrange the fish on a serving plate with the grapefruit segments and tomatoes. Scatter over the chilli and mint, season and drizzle with the oil to serve.

Olive & Orange Seared Tuna

SERVES 4–6
PREPARATION TIME 10 minutes
COOKING TIME 4–6 minutes

500 g (1 lb) thick piece of
fresh tuna
1 teaspoon olive oil, plus extra
to serve
salt and pepper

FOR THE DRESSING
large handful of parsley,
chopped
2 garlic cloves, finely chopped
finely grated rind and juice of
1 orange
50 g (2 oz) green olives, pitted
and chopped

Rub the tuna with the oil and season well. Heat a large
griddle pan until smoking hot, then add the tuna and
cook for 2–3 minutes on each side until browned but
still pink in the centre. Remove from the pan and cut
into small bite-sized cubes.

Meanwhile, make the dressing by mixing together
all the ingredients in a bowl.

Place the tuna on a serving plate, then pour over the
dressing. Drizzle with a little extra olive oil before serving.

Trout with Matcha Pistachio Crumb

SERVES 2
PREPARATION TIME 15 minutes
COOKING TIME 8–10 minutes

25 g (1 oz) raw unsalted
  pistachios
1 teaspoon matcha
  powder
1 tablespoon breadcrumbs
1 tablespoon olive oil
1 lime, zested then sliced
1 large or 2 small whole
  rainbow trout, gutted and
  cleaned (ask your
  fishmonger to do this)

small handful of soft herbs,
  such as parsley, chives or
  coriander
sea salt and ground black
  pepper

TO SERVE (OPTIONAL)
75 g (3 oz) mixed salad leaves
100 g (3½ oz) heritage
  tomatoes, thickly sliced
extra virgin olive oil

Put the pistachios, matcha powder and breadcrumbs into a food processor and blitz for about 10 seconds until the pistachios are crumb-like, but not too fine. Mix with the olive oil and lime zest.

Put the trout on a baking tray lined with baking paper. With a sharp knife, make 3 diagonal slits along the top of the fish. Season generously and stuff the cavity with any herbs you wish, plus the lime slices.

Press the matcha pistachio crumb all over the top of the trout, reserving some for the salad, if making.

Roast in a preheated oven 200°C, (400°F), Gas Mark 6, for 8–10 minutes until the fish is opaque in the middle.

Serve with a tomato salad, if liked. Arrange the salad leaves and sliced tomatoes in a bowl, scatter over the reserved pistachio crumb and drizzle with olive oil.

Turmeric & Tamarind Cod

SERVES 2
PREPARATION TIME 10 minutes + marinating
COOKING TIME 8 minutes

1 tablespoon tamarind paste
½ teaspoon grated fresh turmeric or ground turmeric
1 tablespoon hot water
2 x 200 g (7 oz) skin-on cod fillet pieces (ask the fishmonger to remove any bones)
½ onion, grated
good splash of rose or jasmine tea
lime wedges, to serve

FOR THE SALAD
½ white cabbage, finely chopped or grated
½ small cucumber (ideally Lebanese), sliced
½ red onion, thinly sliced
handful of soft fresh herbs, such as basil, mint or dill
1 teaspoon black onion seeds
2 teaspoons manuka honey or raw honey
3 tablespoons natural yogurt
sea salt and ground black pepper

Mix the tamarind paste, turmeric and hot water in a large bowl until combined, then set aside to cool. Toss the fish in this marinade, then add the onion and chill in the refrigerator for 20 minutes.

Toss all of the salad ingredients together in a bowl until well combined. Season with salt and pepper and set aside.

Heat a nonstick frying pan over a high heat, then place the cod skin-side down. Cook for 3 minutes, then turn the fish over and add a splash of tea. After the initial whoosh of the tea hitting the pan, reduce the heat, cover the pan and steam for about 5 minutes.

Pile the salad onto plates and top with the fish. Serve with lime wedges alongside for squeezing.

Sole with Matcha Beurre Blanc & Greens

SERVES 2 to share
PREPARATION TIME 15 minutes
COOKING TIME 15–18 minutes

FOR THE MATCHA BEURRE BLANC
½ garlic clove, sliced
1 shallot, thinly sliced
1 lemongrass stalk, crushed
2.5 cm (1 inch) piece of root ginger, peeled and sliced
200 ml (7 fl oz) white wine
60 ml (2½ fl oz) white wine vinegar
1 teaspoon matcha powder
350g (12 oz) chilled butter, diced
squeeze of lemon juice
sea salt

FOR THE SOLE & GREENS
1 tablespoon vegetable oil
1 Dover or lemon sole, skinned and trimmed but kept whole
100 g (3½ oz) curly kale, thickly sliced
100 g (3½ oz) cavolo nero, thickly sliced

Make the matcha beurre blanc. Put the garlic, shallot, lemongrass, ginger, wine, vinegar and matcha powder into a saucepan and bring to the boil. Simmer until the liquid has reduced by two-thirds.

Remove the lemongrass and reduce the heat to low, then add the butter one piece at a time, making sure each addition has been fully incorporated before adding the next.

Strain out the remaining ingredients through a fine-mesh sieve and you should be left with a thickened, glossy liquid. Add a squeeze of lemon juice and season to taste. Keep the sauce somewhere warm to stop the butter solidifying.

For the fish, heat oil in a large frying pan over a medium heat. When hot, add the sole, skin-side down. Leave for 3–4 minutes, depending on size, until golden, then turn over and cook for another 2–3 minutes.

Meanwhile, steam the greens for about 3–4 minutes until just cooked.

Make a bed of the greens on a large plate and place the sole in the middle. Coat the fish in the beurre blanc, making sure the greens get a liberal coating too.

Tomato Stew with Clams & Chorizo

SERVES 4
PREPARATION TIME 15 minutes
COOKING TIME 20–25 minutes

300 g (10 oz) chorizo sausage, cut into chunks
1 teaspoon coriander seeds, crushed
1 tablespoon fennel seeds, crushed
1 onion, finely chopped
1 red chilli, deseeded and finely chopped

2 garlic cloves, crushed
50 ml (2 fl oz) white wine
400 g (13 oz) can chopped tomatoes
200 ml (7 fl oz) fish stock
500 g (1 lb) live clams, cleaned (discard any that don't shut when tapped)
basil leaves, to garnish

Heat a large saucepan over a high heat, add the chorizo and fry until the natural oil has been released and the chorizo is starting to colour. Remove from the pan using a slotted spoon, leaving behind the excess oil, and set aside.

Fry the coriander and fennel seeds in the chorizo oil for 1 minute, then add the onion and chilli and fry until the onion has softened but not coloured. Add the garlic and fry for a further 1 minute. Pour in the wine and bubble until reduced to 1 tablespoon.

Add the tomatoes and stock, bring to the boil and return the chorizo to the pan. Tip in the clams, cover and cook over a medium heat until the clams have opened. Discard any that remain closed.

Scatter the stew with a few basil leaves and serve with crusty bread.

Pork Empanadillas

MAKES 8
PREPARATION TIME 15 minutes + cooling
COOKING TIME 35 minutes

3 tablespoons olive oil
250 g (8 oz) minced pork
1 onion, finely chopped
2 garlic cloves, crushed
3 tomatoes, roughly chopped
2 teaspoons tomato purée
1 teaspoon hot smoked
  paprika

1 roasted red pepper from a
  jar, drained and chopped
500 g (1 lb) ready-made puff
  pastry
flour, for dusting
beaten egg yolk, to glaze
salt and pepper

Heat half the oil in a frying pan, add the mince, season and fry for 5 minutes, breaking up the clumps, until browned. Remove from the pan and set aside.

Add the remaining oil and onion to the pan and cook for 5 minutes until softened, then add the garlic and cook for 30 seconds. Add the tomatoes, tomato purée and paprika and cook for a further 5 minutes until pulpy. Return the mince to the pan with the pepper, stir through and continue to cook for 10–12 minutes, then leave to cool.

Roll out the pastry on a lightly floured work surface until about 5 mm (¼ inch) thick. Using a plate, cut out 8 x 15 cm (6 inch) circles, rerolling the trimmings as necessary. Spoon a little of the pork mixture onto one half of each circle. Brush around the edges with the egg yolk. Fold over the pastry, press out any air, then seal the edges with a fork. Brush with more egg.

Place the pastries on a large baking sheet. Bake in a preheated oven, 200°C (400°F), Gas Mark 6, for 15 minutes, or until golden and crisp.

Matcha Burgers

SERVES 4
PREPARATION TIME 15 minutes + freezing
COOKING TIME 1 hour 50 minutes + resting

FOR THE ONION JAM
30 g (1 oz) butter
220 g (8 oz) red onion, sliced
1 tablespoon balsamic vinegar

FOR THE BURGERS
1 onion, finely chopped
1 teaspoon olive oil, plus extra
  for frying
2 teaspoons matcha powder
400 g (14 oz) minced beef
1 egg
1 tablespoon Dijon mustard
1 tablespoon Worcestershire
  sauce
pinch of sea salt

TO SERVE
4 slices of Cheddar (optional)
4 brioche buns, halved and
  lightly toasted
10 g (⅓ oz) unsalted butter
80 g (2¾ oz) baby spinach
1 avocado, peeled, stoned
  and sliced
pea shoots or salad leaves

Make the onion jam. Heat a saucepan and melt the butter. Add the onion and the vinegar. Cook over a low heat for 1½ hours, until the onions are very soft and jam-like.

For the burgers, sauté the onion in the oil for about 10 minutes over a low–medium heat until soft and translucent, stirring in the matcha powder after 2 minutes.

Tip the onion into a bowl, add the other burger ingredients and combine thoroughly with your hands. Divide into 4 patties, cover with clingfilm and place in the freezer for 10 minutes.

Heat a little olive oil in a griddle pan until very hot. Cook 2 burgers at a time, cooking for 3–4 minutes on each side, depending on how you like your burger. Flip the burgers, add a slice of cheese on top, if using, then let it melt.

Heat a frying pan and add the butter. Sauté the spinach over a high heat for a minute.

Rest the burgers for a couple of minutes before serving in the brioche buns with the onion jam, spinach, avocado and pea shoots or salad leaves.

Bacon, Lettuce & Matcha Salad

SERVES 4
PREPARATION TIME 15 minutes
COOKING TIME 2 hours

1 teaspoon unsalted butter
4 slices of streaky bacon, cut
   into 2.5 cm (1 inch) slices
2 Little Gem lettuces,
   leaves separated
1 ripe avocado, peeled, stoned
   and cut into small pieces
3 hard-boiled eggs, halved

FOR THE DRESSING
100 g (3½ oz) Greek yogurt
1 teaspoon matcha powder
zest and juice of ½ lime
1 teaspoon ume shiso
   seasoning or cider vinegar

FOR THE MATCHA CRISPS
1 potato
2 tablespoons olive oil
1 teaspoon matcha salt

TO SERVE
Parmesan shavings
handful of pea shoots
2 spring onions, sliced

Make the dressing. Combine all the ingredients in a bowl, adjusting the flavour to taste. Set aside.

To make the matcha crisps, slice the potato as thinly as possible with a mandolin or sharp knife. Pat dry with kitchen paper, then toss in the oil and matcha salt. Tip onto a baking tray and bake in a preheated oven, 150°C (300°F), Gas Mark 2–3, for 2 hours, turning over halfway through, until golden. Remove from the oven and rest for 10 minutes to continue crisping up.

In the meantime, heat a frying pan and melt the butter. Add the bacon and cook until crisp.

Put the lettuce leaves into a large mixing bowl and gently combine with the dressing until evenly coated. Place in a serving plate, then add the avocado, bacon, eggs and matcha crisps.

To serve, sprinkle over the Parmesan, pea shoots and spring onions.

Something
Sweet

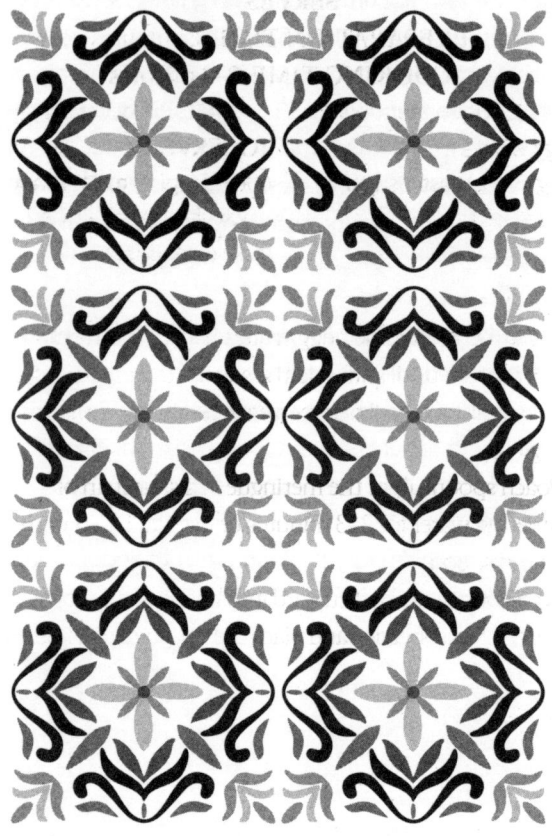

Floating Islands with Raspberries

SERVES 4
PREPARATION TIME 15 minutes
COOKING TIME 2–3 minutes

2 egg whites
100 g (3½ oz) caster sugar

TO SERVE
600 ml (1 pint) ready-made
    vanilla custard, chilled
fresh raspberries

In a clean bowl, whisk 2 egg whites using a hand-held electric whisk until stiff. Add the sugar, 1 tablespoon at a time, whisking well between each addition, until firm and glossy.

Poach spoonfuls of the meringue in a saucepan of simmering water for 2–3 minutes until firm. Drain with a slotted spoon.

Pour a little warmed custard into bowls, scatter over some fresh raspberries and place the poached meringues on top.

Scone & Berry Boozy Trifle

SERVES 4
PREPARATION TIME 15 minutes

250 g (8 oz) strawberries, hulled and quartered, plus extra, halved, to decorate
125 g (4 oz) raspberries
4 tablespoons strawberry or raspberry conserve

4 plain scones, roughly chopped
6 tablespoons dry sherry
600 ml (1 pint) ready-made vanilla custard, chilled
400 ml (14 fl oz) crème fraîche

Place the strawberries, raspberries and conserve in a bowl. Mix well, then transfer to a trifle bowl.

Scatter the scones over the top of the fruit and conserve, then drizzle with the sherry.

Pour over custard, then spoon over the crème fraîche. Decorate with strawberries.

Scone & Clotted Cream Trifles

SERVES 4
PREPARATION TIME 10 minutes

175 g (6 oz) strawberries, hulled and quartered, plus 2 extra, halved, to decorate
4 tablespoons strawberry jam

4 tablespoons clotted cream
2 plain scones, halved

Place the strawberries in a bowl and mix with the strawberry jam. Divide half the strawberries between serving glasses and top each with a spoonful of the cream and then a scone half.

Spoon over the remaining strawberries, then decorate each trifle with a strawberry half.

Lemon-Berry Vanilla Cream Tart

SERVES 4
PREPARATION TIME 10 minutes

200 g (7 oz) lemon curd
1 ready-made sweet pastry
    tart case
    (about 23 cm / 9 inches)
    in diameter

250 g (8 oz) strawberries,
    hulled and sliced
1 vanilla pod, split lengthways
200 ml (7 fl oz) double cream
1 tablespoon icing sugar, sifted

Spread the lemon curd over the base of the tart case,
then scatter over the strawberries.

Scrape the seeds from the vanilla pod into the cream
with the icing sugar and whip until it forms soft peaks.
Spoon over the strawberries and serve immediately.

Mixed Berry Eton Mess

SERVES 4
PREPARATION TIME 10 minutes

400 g (13 oz) mixed berries, such as blackberries, raspberries, blueberries, plus extra to decorate

400 ml (14 fl oz) strawberry yogurt

300 ml (½ pint) crème fraîche

4 tablespoons icing sugar, sifted

4 meringue nests, roughly crushed

Place half the berries in a food processor or blender and blend until smooth. Transfer to a bowl with the strawberry yogurt and stir to mix well.

Mix the remaining berries in a bowl with the crème fraîche and icing sugar. Add to the berry and yogurt mixture and swirl through to create a marbled effect.

Fold the meringue into the mixture and spoon into chilled dessert glasses.

Serve immediately, decorated with berries.

Matcha Eton Mess

SERVES 4
PREPARATION TIME 20 minutes
COOKING TIME 2 hours + cooling

FOR THE MERINGUES
1 egg white
pinch of sea salt
230 g (8 oz) caster sugar

FOR THE SAUCE
270 g (9¾ oz) fresh raspberries,
    washed and patted dry
1 teaspoon honey
250 ml (9 fl oz) double cream
2 teaspoons matcha powder,
    plus extra for dusting
20 g (¾ oz) caster sugar

Make the meringues. Put the egg white into a clean bowl with the salt and whisk to soft peaks. Add half the sugar and whisk to blend well. Add the remaining sugar and whisk again until the mixture is thick and shiny and holds stiff peaks.

Dollop large spoonfuls of meringue onto a baking tray lined with baking parchment, flattening them slightly with the back of the spoon. Bake in a preheated oven, 140°C (275°F), Gas Mark 1, for 2 hours until the meringues are completely dry and crisp on the outside (they will still be a bit squishy in the middle) and can be lifted off the paper easily. Transfer to a wire rack and leave to cool in a dry place.

Make the sauce. Blitz 150 g (5½ oz) of the raspberries with the honey in a blender until you have a smooth sauce, then set aside.

Gently whisk the cream, matcha powder and sugar together until it is very lightly whipped.

Break the meringues into bite-sized pieces and place on a serving platter. Top with the matcha cream, raspberry sauce and the remaining raspberries. Dust with matcha powder before serving.

Lemon Panna Cotta & Raspberries

MAKES 6
PREPARATION TIME 10 minutes
+ chilling and marinating
COOKING TIME 5 minutes

600 ml (1 pint) double cream
100 g (3½ oz) caster sugar
pared rind of 2 lemons
1 vanilla pod, split lengthways
and seeds removed
350 ml (12 fl oz) milk

3 teaspoons powdered
gelatine
100 g (3½ oz) fresh raspberries
5 mint leaves, roughly
chopped
3 tablespoons grappa

Put the cream, sugar, lemon rind and vanilla seeds in a saucepan. Bring to the boil over a low heat, then remove from the heat and leave to infuse for 5 minutes.

Meanwhile, bring the milk to the boil in a separate saucepan. Remove from the heat and carefully sprinkle with the gelatine, in as thin and even a layer as you can manage. Leave to stand for 2–3 minutes until the gelatine no longer looks dry, then stir to dissolve.

Strain the infused cream through a sieve into the milk, stir, then and pour the mixture into 6 x 175 ml (6 fl oz) dariole moulds. Cover each with clingfilm and chill for at least 5 hours until set. The panna cotta will keep for up to 3 days in the refrigerator.

Combine the raspberries, mint and grappa in a bowl. Cover and leave to marinate at room temperature for 30 minutes and up to 4 hours.

Unmould the panna cotta by carefully dipping the base and sides of the moulds in warm water for a few seconds. Invert onto plates and serve with the marinated raspberries.

Apple & Raspberry Grilled Crumbles

MAKES 4
PREPARATION TIME 10 minutes
COOKING TIME 2 minutes

400 g (13 oz) can or jar apple pie filling
100 g (3½ oz) fresh raspberries
8 tablespoons granola crunchy oat cereal
2 tablespoons ground almonds
25 g (1 oz) unsalted butter
vanilla ice cream, to serve (optional)

Mix the apple pie filling with the raspberries and divide between ramekins.

Mix the cereal with the ground almonds, then top with the apple mixture.

Dot with the butter and cook under a preheated medium grill for 2 minutes until warm.

Serve immediately with vanilla ice cream, if liked.

Crunchy Blackberry & Apple Crumbles

MAKES 4
PREPARATION TIME 15 minutes
COOKING TIME 20 minutes

juice of ½ lemon
625 g (1¼ lb) Bramley apples,
   peeled and chopped into
   small chunks
200 g (7 oz) blackberries
175 g (6 oz) demerara sugar

250 g (8 oz) butter
250 g (8 oz) plain flour
125 g (4 oz) muesli
50 g (2 oz) soft brown sugar
custard, to serve

Squeeze the lemon juice over the apples and mix well.

In four 300 ml (½ pint) ramekins, layer the apples with the blackberries and demerara sugar.

Make the crumble topping by rubbing the butter into the flour in a large bowl until it resembles breadcrumbs. Mix in the muesli and soft brown sugar and stir.

Scatter the crumble topping evenly over the fruit. Bake in a preheated oven, 200°C (400°F), Gas Mark 6, for 20 minutes, or until the fruit is cooked and bubbling juices seep through the topping.

Cool for a few minutes and serve with custard.

Apple & Blackberry Crumble Slab Pie

SERVES 8
PREPARATION TIME 20 minutes
COOKING TIME 1 hour 10 minutes–1 hour 15 minutes
+ cooling

FOR THE PASTRY
175 g (6 oz) plain flour
110 g (3¾ oz) cold butter,
    cubed, plus extra for
    greasing
75 g (3 oz) ground almonds
60 g (2¼ oz) icing sugar
finely grated zest of 1 orange
pinch of salt
2 tablespoons cold water

FOR THE CRUMBLE
90 g (3¼ oz) cold butter, cut
    into small cubes
50 g (2 oz) plain flour
75 g (3 oz) light brown sugar
50 g (2 oz) porridge oats
20 g (¾ oz) pecan nuts,
    roughly chopped
1 teaspoon ground cinnamon
pinch of salt

FOR THE FILLING
2 Granny Smith apples,
    peeled, cored and grated
400 g (13 oz) blackberries
2 tablespoons caster sugar

Grease a deep baking tray about 25 x 20 cm (10 x 8 inches) with a little vegan butter and line the tray with nonstick baking paper.

Make the pastry. Put the flour in a large bowl, add the vegan butter and rub it in with your fingertips until the mixture resembles coarse breadcrumbs. Stir in the ground almonds, icing sugar, orange zest and salt.

Mix in the measured cold water until the mixture starts to form clumps, then bring it together with your hands and briefly knead into a smooth ball of dough.

Press the dough evenly over the base of the prepared tray and up the sides a little way and prick it all over with a fork. Bake in a preheated oven, 190°C (375°F), Gas Mark 5, for about 20 minutes until golden brown.

Meanwhile, make the crumble. Using the same bowl, rub the vegan butter into the flour as for the pastry.

Stir in the remaining crumble ingredients. Clump together some of the mixture to form large chunks, leaving the rest relatively fine in consistency.

Make the filling. Mix the apples and blackberries together in a bowl.

Take the pastry out of the oven and leave to cool for 15 minutes. Leave the oven on. Then spread the apple mixture in an even layer and scatter the sugar over the fruit. Sprinkle over the crumble evenly. Bake for 40–45 minutes until the crumble is golden brown and the fruit mixture is bubbling through. Leave to cool for 10 minutes before slicing and serving.

Watermelon & Choc-Chip Sorbet

SERVES 4–6
PREPARATION TIME 20 minutes
+ chilling and freezing
COOKING TIME 5 minutes

750 g (1½ oz) peeled
watermelon, deseeded
and cubed
300 g (10 oz) caster sugar
8 tablespoons lemon juice

pink food colouring (optional)
1 egg white
125 g (4 oz) chocolate chips

Purée the watermelon in a food processor or blender. Add the sugar and process for 30 seconds.

Pour into a saucepan and bring slowly to the boil, stirring until the sugar has dissolved, then simmer for 1 minute. Remove from the heat, add the lemon juice, then leave to cool, adding a few drops of pink food colouring, if liked. Chill for at least 1 hour or overnight.

Use an ice-cream machine for the best results. Half-freeze the mixture according to the manufacturer's instructions, then lightly whisk the egg white and add with the motor still running. Stir in the chocolate chips, then transfer to a plastic freezerproof container and freeze until firm.

Alternatively, freeze the mixture in a shallow freezer tray until frozen around the edges, then mash well with a fork. Whisk the egg white until stiff in a bowl. Drop spoonfuls of the sorbet into the egg white while whisking constantly with a hand-held electric whisk until the mixture is thick and foamy. Return to the freezer to firm up, then stir in the chocolate chips when almost frozen. Freeze until firm.

Transfer the sorbet to the refrigerator for 20 minutes before serving to soften. Serve with dessert biscuits.

Lemon Sorbet

SERVES 4
PREPARATION TIME 20 minutes
+ cooling and freezing
COOKING TIME 5 minutes

6 lemons
250 g (8 oz) caster sugar

375 ml (13 fl oz) water
2 egg whites

Remove the rind from 2 of the lemons using a vegetable peeler and squeeze the juice into a bowl. Set aside the juice and place the rind in a saucepan with the sugar. Pour in the measurement water and cook until the sugar has dissolved. Leave to cool.

Very slightly trim one end of the 4 remaining lemons so that they stand upright, then cut off the tops. Scoop out the flesh and squeeze the juice into the reserved lemon juice. Place the lemon shells in the freezer.

Add all the lemon juice to the cooled sugar syrup, then pass through a sieve. Place the syrup in an ice-cream machine and churn following the manufacturer's instructions.

When the sorbet is almost frozen, whisk the egg whites in a clean bowl until soft peaks form. Transfer the sorbet to a bowl and beat, then stir in one-third of the whisked egg whites. Gradually stir in the remaining whites in 2 batches. Spoon the mixture into the frozen lemon shells and place in the freezer until frozen.

Matcha Lollipops

MAKES 6 lollipops
PREPARATION TIME 15 minutes + freezing

500 g (1 lb) Greek yogurt
with honey
2 teaspoons matcha powder
½ teaspoon vanilla extract

100 g (3½ oz) white chocolate,
broken into pieces
2 teaspoons cacao nibs
2 teaspoons hazelnuts,
crushed

Whisk together the Greek yogurt, matcha powder and
vanilla extract until thoroughly combined.

Divide the mixture between the lolly moulds. Insert a
wooden lolly stick into the centre of each mould and
freeze for at least 6 hours.

Before serving, melt the chocolate in a heatproof bowl
set over a saucepan of barely simmering water. Stir until
melted, then set aside.

Take the lolly moulds out of the freezer and hold under
the cold tap for a few seconds until you can release the
lollies from them. Dip into the melted chocolate or, using
a spoon, drizzle the chocolate over the sides. Sprinkle
with the cacao nibs and hazelnuts.

Serve as soon as the chocolate sets.

Iced Watermelon, Lime & Grenadine Coolers

MAKES 4
PREPARATION TIME 10 minutes

½ watermelon
50 ml (2 fl oz) grenadine
50 g (2 oz) caster sugar

15 g (½ oz) mint leaves, chopped
finely grated zest and juice of 1 lime

Whizz the watermelon in a blender with the grenadine, sugar, mint and the juice and zest of the lime.

Fill tall glasses with crushed ice, pour over the watermelon mixture and serve immediately.

Frozen Bellini

SERVES 4
PREPARATION TIME 15 minutes

750 g (1½ lb) ripe peaches,
  stoned
100 ml (3½ fl oz) sweet
  sparkling wine

juice of ½ lemon
1 tablespoon icing sugar,
  plus extra to taste
15 ice cubes

Put 500 g (1 lb) of the peaches in a blender and blend to a purée. Transfer to a large bowl. Slice the remaining fruit, put in a separate bowl and gently toss with the wine.

Whizz the lemon juice, icing sugar and ice cubes in the blender until the ice is well crushed – you may need to do this in stages to avoid overheating the blender.

Transfer the crushed ice mixture to the bowl with the fruit and stir well to combine thoroughly. Taste, adding more icing sugar if necessary, and serve immediately, topped with the sliced fruit.

Recipes Index

**Recipes are marked as
being suitable for vegans
(vg) or vegetarians (v)**

UK/US Glossary

aubergine.................................eggplant

baking tray.........................baking sheet

barbecue...grill

beetroot...beets

biscuit..cookie

broad beans...........................fava beans

chilli...chili

chilli flakes.................red pepper flakes

clingfilm...............................plastic wrap

coriander...................................cilantro

cos lettuce ....romaine lettuce

courgette...................................zucchini

cream (double)................. heavy cream

cream (single) ....light cream

crisps..chips

flour (plain)............................all-purpose

flour (self-raising)....................self-rising

flour (wholemeal)...........whole-wheat

frying pan ....skillet

greaseproof paper................wax paper

grill..broil

jam...jelly

jug ....pitcher

kitchen paper ....paper towels

lolly...popsicle

natural yogurt...................plain yogurt

pastry case ....pie case

pepper (green/red/yellow)...............

....bell pepper

porridge oats.........................oatmeal

prawn...shrimp

ridicchio...................................chicory

rocket...................................... arugula

sieve..strainer

sorbet.......................................sherbert

spring onion ....scallion

stoned..pitted

sugar (caster)............................superfine

sugar (icing)..................confectioners'

sweetcorn.......................................corn

tart...pie

tomato purée..................tomato paste

Publisher's note:

Standard level spoon measurements are used in all recipes.
1 tablespoon = one 15 ml spoon
1 teaspoon = one 5 ml spoon

Both imperial and metric measurements have been given in all recipes. Use one set of measurements only and not a mixture of both.

Eggs should be medium unless otherwise stated. The Department of Health advises that eggs should not be consumed raw. This book contains dishes made with raw or lightly cooked eggs. It is prudent for more vulnerable people such as pregnant and nursing mothers, the elderly, babies and young children to avoid uncooked or lightly cooked dishes made with eggs. Once prepared these dishes should be kept refrigerated and used promptly.

Milk should be full fat unless otherwise stated.

Fresh herbs should be used unless otherwise stated. If unavailable use dried herbs as an alternative but halve the quantities stated.

Ovens should be preheated to the specific temperature – if using a fan-assisted oven, follow manufacturer's instructions for adjusting the time and the temperature.

Pepper should be freshly ground black pepper unless otherwise stated.

This book includes dishes made with nuts and nut derivatives. It is advisable for customers with known allergic reactions to nuts and nut derivatives and those who may be potentially vulnerable to these allergies, such as babies and children with a family history of allergies, to avoid dishes made with nuts and nut oils. It is also prudent to check the labels of pre-prepared ingredients for the possible inclusion of nut derivatives.

Vegetarians should look for the 'V' symbol on a cheese to ensure it is made with vegetarian rennet.

Also Available

Recipes for Pickling & Preserving

Recipes for Savoury Bakes

Recipes for Soups